Why didn't they tell me

KENNETH ZIFER

Copyright © 2021 by Kenneth Zifer

All rights reserved.

ISBN:

WHY DIDN'T THEY TELL ME

As I look back in time, I see now the darkness and the light. I was born on 08 – 25 – 1946 and weighed 3 lbs. 6 oz and my parents said I had high fevers and pneumonia and the Doctors gave me heavy doses of penicillin and terramycin and sent me home. My Grandparents Zifer / Zafaro were born in "Calabria Italy" and had Jewish blood. The High Priest at the Temple in Jerusalem Israel fled with all the Jewish Priest and their families in 70 AD to Calabria Italy. In Solomons Temple there were over "25,000 Jewish Priests" and the Jewish families had 6 to 8 children. Then on my mother's side my Grandparents were from Germany and their name is spelled different, Rieger and there were "73 Rieger's" that went through the "Holocaust" and one was a Jewish Rabbi. So, my families prayed, and the fevers broke. Then my Mom told me when I was 2 years old the fevers came back, and she took me to a Doctor her Dad was going to for crippling arthritis. The Doctor had a $ 250,000 dollar machine that diagnosed infirmities. The Doctor sent me home and said he has mucus on his left lung take some fresh parsley and make a tea with it and have him drink it and the fevers left. Then when I was 4 years old, I accidently swallowed a copper lamp out of a gum ball machine at Grandmas store. Mom took me to our local MD Dr. Bennet, and he checked me and said the copper lamp was in the side of my stomach and I would not pass it which meant an operation. Dad said no operation, take him back to Doctor Robinson with the machine. It was 100 miles away, so Mom took me. Now I remember what he looked like, and he stood in front of me with a wand in his hand and the other hand he moved his hand in a circular motion on the table as there were big meter dials on it and the cord connected to it. Doctor Robinson told Mom he had moved it and take some sewing thread and wrap several wraps on some gum and have him swallow it so it will pass. Well, I didn't tell Mom when I went to the bathroom and she took me back to the MD and Doctor Bennet checked me and said I passed it. Thank you, Jesus. In the 3rd grade me and my cousin were drummers in the high school marching band and when I watched our first cousin Sonny Zifer QB and Gene Zuchegno RB another first Cousin playing, there was so much excitement at the football games listening to the name Zifer and Zuchegno on the PA system as our band watched from the bleachers and went on the field at half time to march and play, this excitement encouraged me to go out for middle school football. Before this happened, we moved to the country called Dundee, Ohio in 1956 where we lived in a two-story Amish Farmhouse and I would go and help the farmers take in hay. They took it in loose with a team of Draft horses this is where I learned to drive a team of horses taking in hay. Then Dad built a new home for us in Winfield, Ohio where we helped the farmers loaded hay bales on a wagon that a Powerful Oliver Tractor pulled the loaded down trailer as the Diesel Inline 6 would win at the Tractor pulls in its class. The farmer we loaded hay for John took me to one of the Tractor pulls. One day John said Ken y'all can have all the sweet corn you want to eat by the cemetery so I would take the wheel barrel and load it down with corn as a 11-year-old gets hungry and I love fresh corn and would eat a dozen ears at a meal. We had a family of 7 so I kept the corn coming. One day John said Ken did you know you are eating field corn as the sweet corn is gone and I said corn is corn and it sure is good. God Blessed us. Dad worked on the Nickle Plate Railroad as an Electrician where they completely overhaled the Big Diesel Locomotives they would rewire the electric motors that drove the wheels and we were back in the High School District to go out for Middle High School football and at the age of 11years old and I found out I had tremendous strength and speed. During these early years of football, I met a Cousin of ours the famous Zuch Zuchegno a running back who ran the 100 yd. dash in 9 sec. and who scored 33 points in one football in high school and 34 TD in a season and continues to hold the State High School Record in Ohio. He received a full scholarship to Ohio State and was their fullback his Sophomore year. In Middle School at the age of 11 years old I was picked Full Back and my cousin Zuchegno was left half back. He amazed me the way he ran the football with moves that the defense had problems with. As a freshman in high school at the age of 13 years old I was a first-string linebacker on the high school football team. How was I able to achieve this being born a preemie? One day walking by the Catholic Church near the school out of the blue sky I said God give me a mate and a beautiful one. Watch what God does. There is a Light of Jesus Christ on the earth and there is a Darkness of Evil on the earth. You can read about it in your Bible about the evil forces and God's Power on the earth.

John 10:10 (KJV)

10 The thief cometh not, but for to steal, and to

kill, and to destroy: I am come that they might

have life, and that they might have it more abundantly.

John 8:44 (KJV)

44 Ye are of your father the devil, and the lusts of your father ye will do. He

was a murderer from the beginning, and abode not in the truth, because

there is no truth in him. When he speaketh a lie, he speaketh of his own:

for he is a liar, and the father of it.

TRANSISTION TO THE GREAT SOUTH
1960

These darkness encounters do take place on the earth. The light encounters will lead you up to a higher calling when you, Repent of your sins and Accept Jesus Christ as your Lord and Savior. In 1960 our Defensive High School Football Coach Wayne Malone would put me in the center of the field and pick the two biggest and strongest players on the field and have the football team form a circle in the middle of the field and he would say I'm going to show you what a smaller player can do. Coach would line me up against these two great players and have me charge through them. Football is a contact sport. The darkness comes in as I was picked first string defensive end my sophomore year and my birth certificate, they said had a problem. Coach Wayne said Ken I hate to tell you this you can't dress out for the first game of the season. Then the next week the same routine in the middle of the field. Come game time Coach Wayne said as he put his arm around me said son the Athletic Director is a Basketball Coach; he cares less about your birth certificate. I had no choice but to leave. There was nothing wrong with my birth certificate, who is the darkness? That same year 1960 prayer was removed in all the schools in America and the Priest and Preachers said nothing about it in the Sanctuary. WHY, WHY, were they quiet? I could not understand this. I started first string my Junior year on Defense and my Senior year held the position of a Running Blocking Back leading interference I was the only one in the school history to hold that position. I played both ways and was the inside linebacker on the left side of defense. God used me in a mighty way to help my Head Coach and Principal Dr. Wayne Malone who was QB for Tn. This is a picture of darkness and light as I will continue to show you. Dr. Wayne Malone offered me the Machine Shop and Welding Course for another year with credits and I'm the only one who received that honor as I built and welded goal post for the High School football field. I would walk ¾ of a mile at night to the Machine Shop to get more experience by welding on almost every horse trailer in Pasco County Fl. to gain more skills in that field. Dr. Wayne Malone had several College Division 2 Scholarships for me, and I thanked him. My hands were so sore after the football games I could hardly move them from the tackles and moving people out of my way on defense. I broke my hand on a tackle with a big pile up on the second game from the season. My parents were very proud as the name Zifer was on the loudspeakers all night long with the other great players. Me and my brother where the two running backs, Ron was a sophomore. Now after I Graduated from High School in Dade City, Florida I chose to gain more skill in the field of welding. I'm headed to get State Certified in all types of welding, arc, heliarc, and gas welding in Orlando Fl. at the Orange County Vocational School. It was a 1 ½ year course and I completed it in 6 months, what realm makes that happen.

THE POWER OF JESUS CHRIST & THE DEMONIC REALM

Our President John F. Kennedy was assassinated in November 1963 and divorce broke out with some of our families as they came under attack and it was a shock to all of us even as a 17-year-old. In 1967 after boot camp a friend of mine in the Army new the famous Smokey Yunick engine builder and race car builder in Deland, Florida. He said come over for the Daytona 500 race Smokey Yunic has his car in the race. Buzzie had told me about Smokey Yunick and said Ken my Dad Emile is the same caliber they called Emile Einstein he developed the first fuel injection for a chevy engine, and he won some big races in Florida. The day of the Race at Daytona in 1967 we were excited to see the famous 1967 Chevelle with the Mystery Engine 427 cui on the pole position. I walked out of the infield on to the racetrack and stood 10 feet from the car and staired at it minutes before the big race. The # 13 Chevelle held the fastest time and Curtis Turner was the driver. The huge engine screamed at a high rpm as it went around the track and I closed my eyes and could point at it from all the race cars. The 426 Hemi of Richard Petty could only get 6 car lengths from the Chevelle with the Mystery Engine. The Mystery Engine took the first 20 laps of the race and made the same amount of money as the 4th place winner. I was helping the famous Buzzie Reutimann 00 racing team as I was assigned to all the welding assignments, roll bars, frame, I was turned loose on building a set of headers for his two Nascar Super Modified 37 Chevy Coupes and I told Buzzie I can arc weld the gas tank for you. He said Ken no one can do that. I said I can, and we will place 40 lb. pressure on the tanks to test them for leaks. No leaks thank you Jesus. Buzzie's two race cars took him to the Nascar Super Modified Hall of Fame thank you Lord. I was working on the Coastline Railroad in Florida on a Big Timbering Gang running the track liner machine and worked at night with the Mechanic from Waycross Ga. as he used my welding skills on all the broken metal parts on the machines. I traveled the whole state of Florida timbering track and running a Dragline with a work train pulling me from Attapulgus Ga. to North Miami seeing wild panthers and gators and swamp and land that most people have never seen. These welding skills that God blessed me with have taken me to help many people and make me a living. I knew God and talked to him as a Catholic and then when I said one day as a 13-year-old, God give me a mate and a beautiful one and as you read, he fulfilled my dream as he opens up doors for me. In 1968 I was invited over to a family to visit and there was a girl that I could not take my eyes off of as she was in the living room by herself when I walked in. I sat down and all I could do is look at her as she was quiet and did not know what to say. I never had this happen to me before. She was so beautiful I could not help myself. We finally talked and her cousin let us go on a date with them. To be honest that is love at first site. We dated for about a year and got married on Jan. 24, 1969 when God opens up doors, he knows how to do it. God is awesome all the time.

I repented of my sins and accepted Jesus Christ as my Lord and Savior in a Missionary Baptist Church in Dade City, Florida and received my Certificate of Baptism on Sept. 13, 1969. I felt good about myself as my wife to be was a Baptist and was Baptized by the same Preacher Johnie in Pretty Pond just like I was. Now what I'm going to show you is what the Lord showed me as you will not be taught by most Preachers or Priest. About two years later as we plowed through the scriptures something happened. The church members voted for Pastor Johnie to be full time Pastor by him moving into a new mobile home trailer on the church property. His wife refused to make the change and they left. Evil does not care who you are and satan and his demons work through people. A couple of years later Pastor Johnie's wife and their oldest child went to prison for Mobile Home Fraud. Johnie died later, and he was not recognizable when he died. He had a long white beard down to his waist and very hairy and he looked like a hermit. satan and his demons do not care who you are, and the darkness moves through the earth. The Power of Darkness hit my Dad and Mom as they got a divorce, and it was a shock to all of us and the rest of the family. On Jan. 24, 1969 me and Cathy were married. In1973 the Federal Law passed Roe v Wade allowing "Abortion / Killing "babies legal in America. The Priest and Preachers were quiet in the Sanctuary about it. WHY, WHY, were they quiet? Do you see the darkness as I continue to reveal it and the Light? In 1972 I was hired on by the Telephone Co. and they sent me to the First Schools they started in Leesburg, Florida. Pole climbing, Installation of phones, Electronic Key Systems, Small PBX Systems and I spent 3 months working with Skilled Techs. Pulling cables in Banks and other Business and working on Mechanical Key Systems. Then I worked on the Line Crew for 6 months hanging aerial cables on Poles as the Industry was growing. Then one day the local Co. needed Repair Technicians, so I raised my hand and volunteered to go on maintenance for local residence. Then the Co. picked me as Head Plant man for Trilacoochee Exchange area as the Withlacoochee River flowed through this small former Logging Town. The title was just a name and my goal in life was to be the best maintenance repairman to give the public the best phone service bar non and make my Supervisors proud. The Reports started coming in and it was told to me by a Christian in the Local Dade City Florida office, and she said don't say anything the Report went to the Vice President of the Co. and the report showed the Trilacoochee Office had the best report for the month in the State of Florida for our Company. It was 83 % out of 100 % points and the Company goal was 82 for the month. I kept it to myself and kept plowing making our customers happy and my Supervisor for 2 ½ years. During that time, I met a famous man called the "Iron Man" from Lachoochee, Florida. As a teenager were heard the true stories about him. The former Sheriff's Sister lived next door to us as we were teens in Dade City, Florida. Norma told us about the Iron Man as she grew up in Lachoochee and he had tremendous strength he could take a solid glass ash tray and crush it in one hand, he would let you take an empty beer bottle and bust him over the head with it, but you had to buy him a beer. Our Line Foreman at work who grew up in the Logging Town of Lacoochee said he saw him line up men on a pay day and he would let them hit him in the chest with an 8 lb. sledgehammer to try and knock him down on the ground and if you couldn't you had to give him your weeks' paycheck. The Constable for the County told me he would use the Iron Man to help him round up the bad guys. He could take a Vanier Block at the Logging Mill and pick up one end of it by himself and it took 4 men to lift the other end of the huge block of wood. He could lift the Railroad Axel and wheels from a Train Box Car putting a chain around the end of the axels and over his shoulders and lift it off the rail. Well, the Lord has put a lot of famous people in my path all my life. I had a trouble ticket in Dec. 1973 and as I was working on the phone for this elderly lady as she was talking to her neighbor, I heard them say the "Iron Man" is back in Town. When I finished my work, I asked them about the Iron Man, and I said where can I see him at, and they said down at Howards Bar in Lacoochee. Well on the way back to the Office driving by Howards I checked the pay phone and Howard came into that location of the building where it was, and I asked He said yes, see that Plymouth parked out there, I said yes. He said that is his car and if you come back after 7:00 pm you can meet him. WOW I was excited. I finished work went home and I told Cathy after I ate, I'm going to meet the Iron Man from Lacoochee, she was concerned, I told her I will be alright. It was close to Christmas and I head up to Lacoochee. I will never forget when I walked in it took me back 100 years in time. It looked older than the Wild West movies we watched on TV. Mack met me and said Ken he is in the back where the pool room is. He took me back there and you had to cut through the smoke in the pool room and I'm looking for some huge man and I did not see one. Then Mack introduced me to him. He was sitting in a chair with an Army Jacket on and when he stood up, I had to look up as he was 6'4 inches tall he said he weighed 220 lbs. and when he shook my hand his had ate up all of my hand it was so huge and long. His hand was almost twice as long as an average big hand. Well, our assignment in Jesus Kingdom is tell people about Jesus and Salvation. On my lunch at work, I would go see him and talk to him. When he first came to Lacoochee from Ga. he said everyone in the logging Industry new his Dad who was 6' 6 inches tall and weighed 300 lbs. He said he could load 55 gal. Oil Drums on a truck by himself. He went on to tell me that he decided to date one of the local women in Lacoochee and the girl's brothers were against it and they came into Town with a Shot Gun to run him off. The Iron Man said Ken I took the Shot Gun from the one brother and put a bend in it over my knee where they could not shoot it. He had another encounter with a man, and I worked with his Son at the phone Company. This man pulled a knife on the Iron Man and he said he took the knife from him and took his thumb and popped the knife blade off. The Iron Man was shot with a 3030 rifle and shot with a 22 rifle. God spared him. One time when I went to see him, he said Ken wait here as he walked out by the road from his house, and he said Bill left this Ax out here. It had a blunt side on one end, and he said watch this, he chocked the end of the Ax handle and swung it out in front of him and drew it back and hit himself in the chest several times as hard as he could, and it did not faze him. Then he said hit me in the chest with your fist. I said I do not want to do that to you, and he said hit me with your fist and I did, and it was like hitting a piece of "WOOD" that is how tough he was when he tensed up. Then he took a cigarette and said Ken light it for me, so I did, and he took the cigarette and held it on his arm and blew it till the end was bright red with fire and burnet a hole in his arm and I said you don't have any fillings do you and he said yes, I do but I do not let them know it. He could take the thick beer mugs and crush them. I talked about the Lord to him, and I helped him get a job at a chicken farm south of Dade City. I went to see him and when I did, he was reading his Bible and he told me he got in trouble all the time for sticking up for a smaller man when someone was going to try and hurt them. The former Police Chief of Dade City told me he used the Iron Man to help them go after a person who broke out of Jail or someone, they need to catch quick. This was in the late 1940's and early 1950's. I was glad to know he accepted Jesus Christ and one day I took my Dad out to see him. The stories were backed up by the local Law Enforcement and the County Constable that worked at the time. The Iron Man worked at the Logging Mill, the "Cummer Sons Cypress Co." who built a full Electric Powered Sawmill, cutting Cyprus trees, Pine trees, and Hardwood trees they had over 45,00 acres next to the Green Swamp of Florida. The Iron Man worked there during the early 1940's. He said Ken I'm going to where my family is in Bartow, Florid and I asked him if he had any Sons that had the strength like he had and he said yes at the time he had a Son that was 12 years old, and he was 6' tall and had strength and another Son in his 30's that was in the Airforce and he had the strength. He told me he was ¾ Cherokee and came out of the Black Foot Tribe and he was ¼ Irish that was on his mother's side. It was an honor to meet him and when he left, he said his wife had remarried. He died about two years later in Bartow Florida while working. He wore a size 13 boot and he showed me pictures in his Restyling Uniform, it was my assignment to make sure he Repented of his Sins and Accepted Jesus Christ. Thank You Jesus for putting the Iron Man in my path. an internal investigation and sent the Companies first Instructor over Pole Climbing and Residential Instalation and he played football as a Fullback at Florida State and he knew I played football and had a lot of respect for me. In 1975 a New Manager was brought in he wore a white suit and tie. I liked what he had to say, the Customer comes first they pay our wages he said I'm here to help all of you, if you have personal problems, I will be glad to help you. I said Lord this is a blessing. As I was still at the assignment, they moved me to, here comes the New Supervisor in his white Tornio Ford vehicle for the area and he said you are in a hurry. I said yes Jim, I'm knocking out these disconnects for you. He said Ken I want you to clean up San Antonio for me, I only have 6 months to change things for the Company. I said I do not want to come under attack for doing too good of work and I can't promise you I can fix the problem there are techs a lot smarter on technical issues than me. He said Ken that will never happen to you again I want you to take the position. I said ok. When you have God on your side anything is possible. No one knew what the problem was in San Antonio at our meeting with the Techs. One said it is the Catholics that is the problem. I sat there and said this Tech is very smart on paperwork and calculations what is that about to myself. So, I headed out to San Antonio Florida and the Lord helped me find the problem. The people were getting cut off on long-distance calls. I found a repeater was not installed to boost up the lines voltage and it stopped the complaints to the Public Service Commission. I had 5 years of working with a Great Supervisor and making people happy, our customers. Jim was forced out over a termination of an employee. He was transferred and what is sad to say years later I went to see him, and he wanted me to come and help him doing office work and that was not my expertise. He ended up taking his life. It hurts me to type this. As a Believer I should have told him about Jesus. He may have been a Christian and did not know about the Darkness of Evil. As I continue to show you a picture about "Good and Evil "it is for real as the Lord shows me in real life situations and what happens on the earth in our daily life and as we get deeper into the subject, I will show you how as a believer you have a way out from the darkness. Yes it is for real and as I continued to study the Holy Scriptures I gained more Heavenly Wisdom what the Light represents and what the Darkness represents as it gets more and more interesting so hang on this journey we are on and share it as what I'm going to show you most Preachers will not tell you as they come out of the Seminary to teach their Doctrine and nothing else, that is all they know and if they go be on that they are moved by the Religious Board Members in their church or they will bring charges to the " Church Overseers ". Yes, that is a wake-up call to most Christians in the body of Christ. The Lord has showed me this and I did not read it in any book, that is why the Lord has stirred my Spirit up to write this book to show how the Darkness comes on the earth and the Light from Jesus Christ is for all Believers who accepted Jesus Christ our "JEWISH RABBI "and his name is Yeshua, and we call him Jesus. In 1983 Dade City picks a New Police Chief Bernie Enlow as the former Police Chief came under investigation by the Florida Department of Law Enforcement. When I met Chief Enlow I had an order to install a new key system for the New Police Station in Dade City and that is how I met him. He was the easiest customer I had to work with. As I was pulling cables for the phone system, I said Chief where do you want these phones located. He said Ken you put them where you think we need them. Wow he was easy to work with. He was 43 years old and retired from the Police Department of Clearwater Florida as Major Enlow with 20 years' service and was picked to go to the "Quantico, Virginia FBI Academy "Training Center. The Clearwater Police Department had over 300 officers on the force. In Sept. 1986 Police Chief Bernie Enlow Dade City, Florida Sponsors Ken and Cathy Zifer in the Police Academy. We were the first married couple to go to the Police Academy in Central Florida. Thank God for my precious wife as she took good notes in class, and I was working full time with the Telephone Co. and the school started at 6:00 pm. It was the best training I ever had even better than the Military. Some of the high lights in the Academy a high official at the Attica State Prison of NY was giving the class about prisoners and I asked him a question, what happens on a" full moon "in the Prison. He said that is a good question, all "hell" breaks out with inmates taking their metal cups and raking the iron bars. Do we see the Darkness and Evil again? We had the State Attorney over Law Enforcement teach us the Laws. He said by the way on the books in the State of Florida for 100 years a person can have sex with a horse or a cow as long as no one watches. Do you see the Darkness and Evil coming out? The Major at the Pasco County Sheriff Department taught us how your rights can be taken away. He was traveling through the State of Delaware as he rented a car and when he came into Delaware, he was pulled over by the State Police. They asked for his driver's license and he asked them what the problem was, and he told them he was the Major with the

Pasco County Sheriff Department in Florida. They said you are under investigation for trafficking drugs. The Major wanted to talk to a Judge, and they refused everything he had to say. They striped the vehicle and found nothing. They said one out of five vehicles with this Rental Co. is trafficking drugs into their State. He said from then on, he has a dog search the car for drugs before he rents one. His rights were taken away as a Major in Law Enforcement. He told us the King of everyone's home is the owner and never forget it. Now it's time for the Firing Range with our Revolvers and a Shotgun. I told Chief Enlow I will win the "Firearms Proficiency Award "for you. By the Grace of God and the Holy Ghost I won the Award for the Dade City Police Department. The Holy Ghost is powerful, more powerful than people think. The Shotgun test was last at the Firing Range, my babe stands 5'2 and when she fired her Shotgun at the target it hit the Officers target next to her and they gave that Officer the points and if that did not happen that Officer would have failed the course because she did not have enough points to qualify on the Range. That female Officer kept her job by the Grace of God. She thanked Cathy many times. Cathy passed with plenty of points on her target. Now it's time to wrestle a wild gator 6' long as the Game Commission of Florida caught one and brought it to the School. We thought it was a joke that we would have to do this after watching a movie about capturing a gator. Yes, we were picked in pairs to catch a live wild gator at the Police Academy in New Port Richey, Florida as the rest of the class watched. We had to tape its mouth shut and turn it loose, then cut the tape loose which was the most dangerous move on the release of the creature. Now the Driving Range Test was next. We went to Tampa, Florida at the Tampa Police Department Driving Range with the Sargent over the Driving Range who was a man with Authority and Strict. The first day the Sargent said now I want you to pair off two to a crusiser and I want you to get up to a speed of 50 mph and then jam on the brakes and come back here. Cathy runs to the cruiser and climbs into the driver's seat, and I said I'm the hotrodder she has no clue of speed. She put the pedal to the metal to the cruiser and scares me and the way we go as we get closer to the end of the driving range, I said Babe we are getting close to the end of the strip. She said I'm not doing 50 mph yet. Lord help us, she jams on the brakes and spins the curser around and heads back to the Sargent over the driving range. We get out and the Sargent comes over to me and said Ken you do not need to be riding with your wife. I know she sacred you. I said yes sir. Now the next day is the Night Driving Test. Cathy said Ken I can't see the cones; we are not supposed to hit them. God's Favor kicks in and the Sargent said to his Staff Cathy's eyes are dilated from being on the firing range. I'm letting her us the overhead lights on her cruiser for the test. My Babe had favor and we passed the Driving Test. Now at the Police Academy we had to watch a video about how to capture a live gator. As we watched the movie the instructor said y'all will be wrestling one. We laughed and thought it was a joke. Wrong after the class they took us outside and the Florida Wildlife Game Commission pulls up with a wild 6' long gator and turns it loose and the Game Officer said I need two of you Officers to capture this gator and tape its mouth shut Wow. Then release it by cutting the tape loose then the next two come forward. Was I nervous as my Babe was picked to place her hand on the gators eyes and tape its mount shut? Then she had to go back down and cut the tape which is dangerous. Thank You for protecting my wife Jesus. The EMS trained us and Tested us. If you score one low grade in the Police Academy you are out. We were taught the most dangerous time in criminal activity was from 11:00 pm to 2:00 am "Calmest Time of the Night "is between 3:00 am and 6:00 am. Now that is very interesting to me because the "Rabbi's "will tell you that God comes out of the Heavens and Roams the earth from 3:00 am to 6:00 am. The Holy Scriptures tell us Jesus prayed the most on the "4th Watch "from 3:00 am to 6:00 am, that is very interesting to me.

Me and Cathy Graduated in 1986 and were State Certified in Law Enforcement for the State of Florida and worked for Chief Enlow and the Florida Highway Patrol some. My fastest ride was with a State Trooper one night in high pursuit in a Plymouth 440 cui Magnum at 11: 30 pm running a speed of 130 mph, thank God I was a Dragracer and around Race Cars as a teenager. Another night riding the interstate the State Trooper pulled across the Interstate and headed back some and crossed the Interstate again and said hold on Ken be alert as these kinds can be dangerous as he pulled behind the vehicle on the emergency lane. He warned the person and came back to our vehicle and we took off. He said Ken he is using his brake lights to draw others to him.

WHY DIDN'T THEY TELL ME JESUS KINGDOM IS ON EARTH

The Bible does not have the word "Coincident "in it. As I grew up in church all my life the things, I just showed you about what takes place in life and there is good and bad, as a Believer we know there is "Evil and Good", and the Lord showed me about the "Evil Demonic Realm" In 1997 we were headed into town and Cathy had placed her pocketbook on top of the car as she was putting things in the car. We headed out and she realized she lost her pocketbook. We turned around and when we got home the phone Rang and a man said I found a pocketbook on the road and picked it up. I said sir that is my wife Cathy's pocketbook I told him where we lived, and he said I will bring it to you. We tried to pay the man, but he would not take any money for it. He said I would like to invite you to our church, and I said we can do that. So, we went to this Southern Baptist Church and it was interesting to hear what the Preacher had to say as he talked about the Power of Jesus Christ and the Apostles. Then on Oct. 3, 1987 a young child was stabbed to death 46 times in a small subdivision down the road from where we lived. She was 9 years old and her Uncle 39 years old was charged with the bite marks on her shoulder and a 17-year-old teen was charged with stabbing her in the head 9 times and 37 times in the chest. They found her body lying in a field behind the subdivision. It shook the community; how can this happen. Cathy was watching a talk show with the "Renowned John Douglas" who was the first one to develop Profiling Serial Killers. Now I'm going to show you the Power of Jesus Kingdom on earth. The Pastor at this Southern Baptist Church said one night the man that is in jail for killing this child is not guilty. I'm the only Preacher in Pasco County that went to see him. The Power of Jesus Kingdom is for real. A Great

Christian Sheriff was elected, and the two murders were found and arrested. Thank You Jesus for teaching us the deeper things and getting us off the milk as a baby Christian.

> Hebrews 5: 13, 14 (KJV)
>
> 13 For everyone that useth milk is unskillful in the word
>
> of righteousness: for he is a babe.
>
> 14 But strong meat belongeth to them that are of full age,
>
> even those who by reason of use have their senses exercised
>
> to discern both good and evil.

Siting in church all my life something happens to me in this Southern Baptist Church in 1998. The Lord revealed to me things I never knew. It is an Honor to be in his Kingdom.

THE REVELATION
THAT PIERCED MY HEART
IN 1998

In January 1998 something happened to me in Bible Study. The Preacher held up the Bible and said see this Book, if you can't believe everything in it then you need to "Throw it in the Trash Can ". I sat there and said to myself, I never heard a Priest or Preacher ever say that. Then the Preacher said open up your Bibles up to John 10: 10 and let's read it. As I'm looking at it the Preacher reads it out loud. He said Jesus said the Thief, that is satan he comes to Steal, and Kill. At that moment in time something "Pierced my Heart "like a dagger and it shook me. I said to myself he comes to Kill me and my Wife and our Son and my Dad and Mom and my brothers and sisters. It penetrated my "Heart, Mind, Soul "like never before. A revelation is when you read a holy scripture many times even hundreds of times and one day when you read it, something happens to you like it just did me. Now when you look back at the "Darkness "you start to understand what the Darkness is. This Evil Force on the earth, where did it come from? How did it get here? God has hidden "Mysteries "all through it and he expects us to research those Mysteries. It is all about repenting of our sins and becoming a Believer in Jesus Christ and reading the Holy Scriptures and following him and what he says. Jesus wants all of us to reach "Souls "for his Kingdom, planting seeds to people and letting them know you are someone different, it is a "High Calling "to Serve him. I'm showing you a picture like a movie what is going on as we live our lives here on earth and I'm here to show you things that no one ever told you and it is from actual events as it is a journey that you will never forget, and you will tell your love ones and children and grandchildren about how Powerful Jesus Christ is on the earth even today.

John 10: 10 (KJV)

The thief cometh not, but for to steal, Kill,

and destroy I am come that they might have

life, and that they might Have it more abundantly.

Job 2 : 2 (KJV)

2. Again there was a day when the sons of God came to present themselves

Before the Lord, and Satan came also among them to present himself before

the Lord.

And the Lord said unto Satan, From whence comest thou? And Satan

answered the Lord, and said, From going to and fro in the earth, and from

walking up and down in it.

MY WHOLE WORLD CHANGED WHEN I RECEIVED A SUPERNATURAL ENCOUNTER WITH JESUS CHRIST IN 1998

A Revival was taking place at our church. So, the first night me and Cathy went to it and the Evangelist was a well-seasoned Preacher. Now let's look at everything into detail, this church had two women that came against two Preachers and ran them off. This Southern Baptist Church was only 3 years old at the time. I did not know this at the time this happened as I told you Cathy lost her pocketbook on the highway going into town and one of the Brothers at the church found it on the highway. This Brother in Christ called us and told us and asked where you live, I will bring the pocketbook to you. So, he did, and we tried to pay him, and he would not take any money. All he asked was will you come to one of our Services and we said we can do that. We thanked him several times. My question about what happened is this. Was this the Holy Ghost that guided us to this church. The New Part Time Pastor was in place when all the movement of God started to take place. There were other movements of God that took place to draw people to this church. Now this is the Power of the Holy Ghost working and this was in 1997 and what happened the Mother Church asked a member who was a Manager for 12 Toco Bell Stores and use to be a Pastor to help fill in until they could find a Pastor and he said he would help. The member ship was down to 13 members as the Pastor God picked started to plow. In one Month, there was 30 people on the roll at church and me and Cathy were part of the 30. Who has the Power to do these kinds of things? God drew people from all over. A Millionaire who had a Business was traveling up the interstate to buy a house and his New Ford truck two days old quit running at the Dade City Exit and they towed him into town, and on the way, he saw this New Baptist Church and ended up buying a house on a Lake near here and him and his wife became members. What kind of Power is that and who does it? At this same Church in 1998, and I'm 49 years old and sat in Church all my life as a Catholic then I met my beautiful wife, Cathy. Remember I asked God to give me a Mate and a Beautiful one when I was 13 years old. God does listen to us and he answered my prayers as I spoke this out walking by the Catholic Church in 1959. My Babe is Beautiful, and I shared with you my Babe was a Baptist and she always told me Ken the only way into heaven is Repenting of your Sins and accepting Jesus Christ as your Savior. She never beat me up for being a Catholic. Hold on for the Journey as I will go into detail what happened, and you will not read about this kind of Power. On the first night of the Revival the Praise Band was in place, a Guitar and Drums and Cymbals and a piano. During that period, they did not have Keyboards. When the Praise and Worship ended the Evangelist came forward and started Ministering out of the Holy Scriptures. He ended in the book of Acts Chapter 16 about Paul and Silas thrown into Prison and they started to Pray and then went into Praise and Worship and something happened during Praise and Worship a "GREAT EARTHQUAKE" hit and the Prison shook, and the shackles came off all the Prisoners and the Prison doors came unlocked, and the Prison Keeper woke up and saw what happened and he drew a sword to kill himself. and Paul led the keeper to the Lord Jesus Christ. The Evangelist ended with an Altar call for Salvation and they went back into Praise and Worship after Altar call. The Service ended for the first night and as me and Cathy were leaving a Brother in Christ walked up to us in this Southern Baptist Church and said Bro. Ken did you fill the Holy Ghost in here tonight. And I said I did not fill anything, but it was a good message. When I heard "Holy Ghost "I wanted to say Holy Ghost what is that? But I kept my composure. Then another Brother walked up and said the same thing and I said I did not fill anything, but it was a good message. Now when the 3 rd. Brother walked up to us and said did you fill the Presence of the Holy Ghost in here tonight. I said I will "Not Lie "in God's House, I did not fill anything, and it was a Good Service. So, we left and when we arrived home when I walked in our house, I walked over to the wall phone and I raised my hands toward heaven, and I said Lord whatever I'm doing wrong change me Lord and let me fill what my Brothers and Sisters are filling. Sometimes you better be careful what you ask God? The next night we entered the church, and we were sitting two rows from the back and Cathy's Grandmother was sitting next to me on my left and Cathy on my right at the end of the pew. The Service started and something happened at the end of the Service after Altar Call. When they went into "Praise and Worship "there was only one man in the Church that would raise his hands toward Heaven during Praise and Worship. He sat on the second row on the left front, and something happened to me. I will break this down, so you know Jesus Christ Power. As the Praise and Worship was taking place I looked up at the front and Bro. Donny had his hands raised up towards heaven and I said that man loves you so do I and some "Boldness" came on me and I spoke it, Lord I have never raised my hands towards heaven before, I'm going to try it. When I did as I closed my eyes something happened. A Tingling Sensation started on the tips of my fingers then Electricity started on my fingertips and it came down my arms and body then a Numbness Sensation came on my body and then a Weightiness Sensation came over my body, I said Lord what is this as I had my eyes closed and hands raised toward heaven, then I said to myself I'm going to see if I can move my arms. I could not move anything it was like I was frozen in time. It was Holy, Holy, Holy, and this lasted for at least 15 minutes or 20 minutes during Praise and Worship. Then as the Praise Music started to slow down and get soft something else happened, the Tingling, Electricity, Numbness, Weightiness, started to lift off my body as the Praise music got soft as I still had my eyes closed. I said Lord I want more of this, then they hit the "Cymbals "and when they did God's Power came down through me so Powerful, I said Lord I can't stand it, it was so Powerful and Holy, Holy, Holy. Then it started lifting off of me when the Praise music got soft again. I said Lord I want more of this and they hit the "Cymbals "again and it came down through me so Powerful, I said Lord I can't stand it. I did not receive the gift of "Tongues" it was Holy, Holy, Holy, this encounter. Then the Praise and Worship music ended. I turned my head to the left and Sister May, Cathy's Grandmother said something happened to you, I said yes, and she said you look like you are ready to start running. I said yes, I'm ready to start running. I knew nothing about running in God's house. I wish I could have gone back in time and asked Sister May what did she see? I did not say anything to her all I did was just turned and looked at her. She saw something different in my "Countenance". When we get to heaven, I can ask her and Jesus. When these "Supernatural Encounters "take place, your flesh tries to comprehend what is taking place. It's called the "Supernatural Realm "where Jesus functions out of. About two Months later something else happened. The Preacher decided to Preach about the "Gift of Tongues". When he ended, he said satan will try and stop you from receiving this Gift. As I was standing in the back with Cathy, I heard what are you going to do when you walk up front and do not receive "Tongues". When I heard that, I said satan get away from me. Then I said Lord give me everything you want me to have, and "BOLDNESS" came on me and I went forward and there were about 4 people lined up and I was waiting for the Pastor to lay hands on me and pray for me as I was waiting three elders were praying for me in Tongues one was Sister B. I was hungry to receive this Gift and I started working my tongue up and down and the Preacher said do not try to imitate Tongues and when he laid hands on me, the Gift of Tongues started coming out of me so Powerful I had to stop so I could catch my breath and continued with it as it was a Powerful moment as I could not stop with it for about 10 minutes. Thank You Jesus for your Power. Jesus told Ananias to lay hands-on Saul so he will get "Healed" and "Filled" with the Holy Ghost. In Feb. 1998 the Brothers at church said Stone is coming to town.

When I heard the name Stone, I said Cathy that is Powerful Name Stone. I said who is he and she said my Uncle Bobby and his friends go see him. He was coming to Brooksville, Florida and I said to Cathy lets go see this Stone fellow. Now the "Anointing "had come on me that no Priest or Preacher never talked about that I was around, here I'm 49 years old when this happened and in Church all my life. We head to Brooksville to this Conference, and it was on a Friday night. The Church was packed, it held 700 people and they said there was 1,000 people there. When Perry came out on the high Platform, we were sitting 4 rows from the front. He had a large neck and I said to myself he must be a former football player. The first thing he said was I'm not a Prophet I'm an Evangelist. Then he said the Lord reveals things to me at times and then paraphrase Amos 3: 7, before God does anything, he "Revealed" his "Secret" to his Servants the Prophets. I looked at my Babe and said "WOW "are we in Church? Then Stone said I'm going to Preach to you tonight about "THE 5 CHAMBERS OF HELL" and the "FALLEN ANGELS ". I looked at Cathy and said WOW. Stone said we have to start in the Holy Scriptures first, so he started plowing in the book of Job and other places in the Bible. Then he said as we just read the Chambers of Hell are in the deep parts of the earth and water surrounds them. Then he said here is the Data I have pulled, the "Bermuda Triangle "is 25,500 feet deep and he said a friend of his was on an Expedition with a famous French Naval Officer, Explorer, Scientist, and Researcher as he headed to the Bermuda Triangle. Across from the Bermuda Triangle is another Chamber in the earth close to Japan.

Amos 3: 7 (KJV)

7 Surely the Lord God will do nothing, but he revealeth

his secret unto his servants the prophets.

THE DEMONIC REALM 1998

When the Explorer and Researcher went down into the deep crevice with the small submarine when he reached the depth of 10,000 feet deep, he resurfaced the submarine. When he got abord the vessel his crew asked him did you see or hear anything different down there. He said I do not want to talk about it. Three days later he sat his crew down and told them what happened. He said when he reached the dept of 10,000 feet deep he started to hear "HUMAN VOICES "and "CHAINS DRAGING ". Let's look at something. Darkness is Evil and Light is Jesus Kingdom. The Bible mentions "LEVIATHAN "the Evil multiheaded Sea Serpent and it comes against God's people and it represents satan. The Deep Chambers of Hell are surrounded by water as you read in the Holy Scriptures. There is a Heaven, and a Hell and Jesus came to save us from Hell as he shed his blood on the cross for all sins. You must Repent of your Sins and accept Jesus Christ as your Savior. What most people sitting in church do not know is our Savior was a "JEWISH RABBI "and his cousin John the Baptist was a "JEWISH PRIEST "and his Mother was the daughter of the High Priest Aron, Moses' brother. Johns Dad was the Priest at the Temple in Jerusalem and his assignment was to burn incense. Remember the Angel appeared to him standing on the right side of the Altar of Incense. All through the Bible we see God's Power as he functions in the "SUPERNATURAL REALM ". Why is it not taught in the Churches as we look around and we see NO Signs, Wonders, Miracles, Salvation? As we get deeper into Jesus Christ Kingdom on earth you will understand what blocks these Powerful movements of Jesus Christ.

Job 41: 1, 7, 15, 31 (KJV)

Canst thou draw out leviathan with a hook? Or his

Tongue with a cord which thou latest down?

Psalms 74: 14 (KJV)

Thou breakest the heads of leviathan in pieces, and gavest him to be meat to the people in habiting the wilderness.

Isaiah 27: 1 (KJV)

In that day the Lord with his sore and great and strong sword shall punish leviathan the piercing serpent, even leviathan that crooked serpent; and he shall slay the dragon that is in the sea.

Jonah 2:

Jonah 2: 2, 6 (KJV)

2 And said, I cried by reason of mine affliction onto the Lord, and he heard me; out of the belly of hell cried I, and thou heardest my voice.

6 I went down to the bottoms of the mountains; the earth with her bars were about me forever: yet hast thou brought up my life from corruption, O Lord my God.

MORE SIGNS AND WONDERS TAKE PLACE

In 2000 God opened up a door. I was asked to film the Services for the church with the Super VHS Camera I was using to film some of the opening scenes for the Documentary we were doing for the Lord, called Wilderness Excursions of Florida. My Spirit would rise in me during Praise and Worship while running the camera. I would raise my hands towards heaven and shout. Then the Preacher said I'm having a Praise and Worship Team come to our church and I filmed the event. Only the Lord can open these kinds of doors. It was Bart Millard who wrote the Song, "I Can Only Imagine" and it was the "First Public" setting singing the Song with his Band "MERCY ME". Bart wrote the song in just 10 minutes. Inspired by the loss of his Dad when he was diagnosed with cancer and his life was transformed by faith. Jesus Christ will draw you to his Kingdom.

John 6: 44 (KJV)

44 No one can come to me unless the Father who sent

me draws him. And I will raise him up on the last day.

A VISION AND DREAM MANNIFESTED IN 1960 THE LORD KNOWS ALL THINGS

In 1973 I was plowing ahead on a "VISOIN and DREAM" I had as a young 13-year-old teen. As we were riding down the road in our 1957 Chevy Station wagon, out of the blue sky I made a comet and said I'm going to build an Airboat like Uncle Ernie Peters. My Dad chuckled about it, but Mom said he will do it. The Lord will give you Visions and Dreams so he can use you in his Kingdom. Remember I accepted Jesus Christ as my Savior in 1969. The Vision began when our Aunt Shirley took me and my brother Ron to the Gulf of Mexico which was about 32 miles from us to a famous Island called "Aripeka, Florida". It was on a Saturday morning and when we arrived at their Campsite the Atmosphere changed as always when we were around Uncle Ernie. They had their Coleman Camp Stove lit cooking and drinking Coffee. Aunt Shirley said Ernie can you take the boys out for a ride. He said let's go so we loaded up on the Airboat and Ernie was a big powerful man at 6' 3 inches tall and weighed 230 lbs. all mussels. I will never forget he reached up and grabbed the tip of the Airboat Propeller on the biggest "WW II Aircraft Engine" inline 6 cylinder and spun the Propeller and the engine fired up. This is what a teen age boy looks forward to, the "Great Outdoors" that God created. It was windy that day and we went out the Bayou and we started to see white caps and Ernie turned the Airboat around and we headed back to the landing. The next trip that Summer we were painting his house for him. As teens we always worked for nothing and just loved to help people. When I was 11 years old and Ron 9 years old, we would load bales of hay for the local farmers for nothing, just to have something to do. We had the strength to do it. The Farmers would feed us a "Smorgasbord" meal for the work. So, Uncle Ernie said let's go fishing put up the paint brushes. So, we did, and he loaded up the big Airboat with the Companys 4 X 4 truck. We went down through an orange grove down to the Lake. He unloaded the Airboat and we headed out trolling for fish at an idle with the big engine. Hear came a man speeding by in an outboard and Ernie said he wants to race us. Reel in your lines so we did, and he said hold on. As we headed across the lake, we came to a sand bar which was only a couple of inches deep at that end of the lake. He said hold on as we stood next to Ernie as he started to pour the coal to the big engine, and I will never forget what we saw. The water formed waves from the Propeller pull the air towards us. This Airboat is one of a kind. The Huge engine has the Propeller behind us where we stood in the boat, we had a huge round screen behind us then the Propeller and Engine. It had a "Tractor Prop" like in an airplane pulling not pushing. The other Airboats all had a Pusher Propeller as the Propeller was at the back of the boat. As the waves kept coming in, all of a sudden, we took off like a rocket and headed back across the lake. The speed boat did not want any of this Airboat as far as racing. Wow what an expericance. Now do you see the "Vision" and God saw what he could do with it. Ernie headed to South Florida to live and the Airboat had a hole knocked in the bottom and was pulled up on the bank behind his house down in the swamp. His brother Clem sold me the engine and a spare. I measured the Airboat end to end as I knew there must be something different about this Airboat. Me and Ron lifted the huge engine which was 56 ½ inches long and the height was 3 ½ feet and it was shaped like a rocket. We lifted the motor by hand out of the old hull. No crane, we were the crane. That is the way we were brought up, This Ended up a 40-year Project for the Lord. I bought a manual from a man in Dade City that flew a WW II Corsair a fighter plane and he had the manual for the Ranger Engine. I found out the best way to time an engine is at night when you can see the piston reach top dead center. I had to go by what I saw and remembered as a 13-year-old and a 23-year-old when I measured the Airboat. I would look at the Aircraft engine for several years and the vision the Lord gave me. One of my friends said Ken you will never get that engine started. I give credit to the Holy Ghost who guided me. I built the hull out of plywood and then fiber glassed it and I built the engine frame out of black iron pipe and built all the brackets for the motor mounts and Johnny Blommel helped me build a bracket to hold the Oil Tank and I used a 1957 gas tank, at the local Machine Shop Mr. Sumner built me a hand crank to start the big engine. I built fish gigs out of stainless steel and placed them on a wooden 1-inch pole. Without the Holy Ghost I'm nothing. We launched the Airboat at Aripeka, Florida at a famous Bayou called Fillmans Bayou where the tide ebbs and flows twice in 24 hours and where the breeding grounds are for the Big Bull Red Fish and the Silver Mullet feed with the Sheep Head and Sea Trout and they gather where the freshwater springs flow into the salt water. This is where we would "FIRE FISH" all night till daylight. In the South Fire Fishing is when you leave your fishing poles at home and take a fish gig and go fishing along the Gulf of Mexico. The Seminole Indians and Miccosukee Tribe would take their wooden cypress canoes and a torch at night to get their main food source fish. The Torch give off light to gig the fish at night, that is where Fire Fishing came from. We run the Airboat for 20 years along the Coast of Florida. People would pull off the highway as we would be getting cooking supplies at a Convenient Store just to look at this one-of-a-kind Airboat, the only one in the World like it. We always came back home with "200 lbs. "of fish. We fed the poor on our journey and had a lot of fun. To give you a view what it was like. I will explain to you the excitement we had as young men. I did not know the Lord was going to use this Documentary to reach Souls for his Kingdom.

THE NIGHT OF THE STORM 1975?

A friend of mine from the phone Co. Bob Owenby a Great Outdoorsman who stood 6' tall and weighed 230 lbs. went on a trip to the Coast with us. He was a strong Believer in Jesus Christ even at work, as he went on Mission Trips to reach Souls for Jesus Kingdom. He built a fish gig out of PVC Conduit which was very light and gave it to our Son Allen. He was deadly with-it gigging fish. We also had the 1964 GMC with the first Big V 6 engine they built. They used that motor in Firetrucks also. We loaded down the truck with firewood, took all the cooking gear. We went to the location where Uncle Ernie use to go and it is called "Fillmans Bayou" it was about two miles from Aripeke along the Coast. When we arrived to drive out on the fill ¼ of a mile long, it was so Overgrown with Bushes and Weeds we had to use an Ax and Machete to get through and I had to have the tied lows and highs down correct as when we arrived at the end of the fill you could only turn around on a low tide. The fill was narrow where we were driving. We set up the Campfire and waited for it to get dusk to light it. I always took 6 people with us. The fishing was great as I would stay out for an hour and then come back to the Camp Fire as the others would be fellowshipping around the fire and drop those off and load up the others and headed back out fire fishing as the "Mean Mother Magnum" lights mounted on the bow shined the bottom of the Coastline. This is where the "Tide Ebbs and Flows" and where the Big Bull Reds breeding grounds are and where the Silver Mullet, Sea Trout, Sheep Head, and Big Bull Sharks feed where the boiling fresh water comes up from the springs and flows into the salt water. It was like riding over a football field as the water was clear and it was a seagrass bottom in areas. One night a huge "Bull Shark" came swimming under my Airboat and that will get your attention. Uncle Ernie Petters would take his crew and drop them off along the Coast with a headlight and a gig pole as they gig fish and others on the Airboat were gigging fish and then he would come back and pick those wading and fishing up. I did not have that desire to do that. One night Ernie ran over Eugene Blommel who was on the Airboat and fell in when he gigs a huge Bull Red Fish, and you just don't stop an Airboat and back up. One night Ernie and Clem and Raymond his brothers had an Airboat load of Red Fish as my friend Bill McKendree saw them coming in from an all-night fishing trip. We gigged Flounder, Red Fish, Trout, Mullet, Sheep Head and we would head back to the campfire and fix baked beans, hush puppies, and throw the fresh fish in the black iron skillet with cooking oil. Wow I'm getting hungry talking about it. It was about 1:00 am and I run the Airboat up on the bank and the rest of the crew was sleeping around the campfire and I found out we forgot the spoons and forks. So, I asked my friend and Bro. in Christ Bob Owenby who was the best dispatcher we had at the phone co. on repair as he could look at the circuit and help guide us. I asked him if he would go with me back to civilization to an all-night store and buy what we needed and headed back. He said yes and as we headed back into town, a "STORM CAME OUT OF THE GULF". As we were headed back from the Store and drove down the fill, I could not see my Airboat, where did it go? I just knew it was out in the Bay somewhere, I was worried about it as this was a long project building it as God Blessed me with the Skills and Heavenly Wisdom and opened doors to do this project. Thank you, Jesus it was in the canal, by the fill as the rise in the tide floated the Airboat off the bank and the storm blew it inward and not out to sea. Thank You Jesus. We ate good as it quite raining, and the crew woke up from their Tarps. We always talked about the Lord on those kinds of trips, and it was great clean fun in the outdoors along the Coast. When we loaded up our Camp Gear and the Airboat, I had to crank up the WW II Aircraft Engine to push the truck up the slippery bank so we could get out of the fishing area and head home. Let's look at something where we also fished at Aripeka, Florida. It is where Babe Ruth, Jack Dempsey, Orville and Wilber Wright, and Winslow Homer stayed on this Island. Ponce de Leon searched for the Fountain of Youth. This is where the Black Bear roams and the Tides Ebb and Flow with the boiling freshwater springs. This is the only place on the Gulf Coast where the water is very clear. This is a rare "Tropical Peninsula where this Project started for the Lord to reach Souls for his kingdom. When you come home you will sleep for two days and if you have problems sleeping you will not after one of our trips to the Coast. As we plowed taking notes what God was doing and him guiding me as we took all the information and stored data what all happened as the Lord wanted me to do a Documentary about the Airboat and talk about how he works through "Insignificant" people on earth when he wants something done to reach Souls for his Kingdom. Every "Believer" in Jesus Christ is on a mission for Jesus Kingdom. It is amazing how if you let God guide you, watch what happens as he functions out of the "Supernatural Realm" and without him I'm nothing. I would like to talk about a fishing trip that ended up in "U S AIRBOAT MAGAZINE" as it was picked as a great adventure in the Outdoors. It happened to us one time in the 20 years fishing along the Gulf of Mexico. It had me praying to the Lord. I will let you decide if there was any Darkness involved or just human error. I will tell you something before I get started. One night two old timers went with us and he gigged his first fish and the fish "Screamed" and it shocked me and he and Allen. That can go down in the record book it was shallow water by a rock it was a "Sheep Head Fish". Was God trying to show me something, I don't know.

THE NIGHT OF THE FULL MOON FRIDAY THE 13TH

This I will never forget, the night of the full moon. I called my friend Bill and I said let's make a run to the Coast Friday night, he said ok. He brought his small Airboat and two friends of ours. We loaded up some firewood and the Airboat and headed to Aripeka and I knew where the Tides were, and it was a "Full Moon". When we pulled up on the Island at 9: 00 pm there were 12 campfire sites with people and their friends. When I backed in the Legend to launch her all the people left their campfires and came over to watch us launch the Big Airboat. They never saw a WW II Aircraft engine with a Tractor Porpeller. A good friend of mine Hank was there and walked down to talk to us and he reminded me it was low tide as I knew. I told Bill if for some reason we do not see your lights on your Airboat we will turn around and come to you. This is some trertrous waters at times with rocks. It was about 3 miles where we were headed to a famous fishing spot called "Philmans Bayou". I run the engine ¼ throttle on the way down and all of a sudden, our Son said Dad I do not see Bill's lights anymore. I did not want to hear that, so I turned around and headed back to find them. As I got closer something did not look wright. As we got closer Bill and his two friends were "Standing" in the Gulf of Mexico. Lord what is going on. They had sunk their Airboat and Bill shouted to me what are we going to do. I said Bill I don't know; the tide is ready to turn, and it will be 3 feet higher. He said Ken there is a "Oyster Bar" not far from us. Can you pull me up to it, I said yes? Now as a Believer the "Holy Ghost" knows all things. Because my Propeller is in front of the engine and not in the back like all Airboats, I can hook onto my frame with a heavy rope I always brought with me, so I tied it off and I told our Son and big John on my Airboat to hold on because I'm going to pour the coal to the Ranger Engine. I put the pedal to the metal, and it

WHY DIDN'T THEY TELL ME

pulled Bill's Airboat which was full of water and that is a lot of weight and I pulled us up on the Oyster Bar. That night was the first time I carried my big tackle box, and I don't know why? We took the lid off and they used it to bail out the water in their boat. Thank You Jesus. Now the best diesel and gas engine mechanic was on Bill's Airboat, Roger. Remember their gas tank was under water. Well Roger started the engine and they said we are ready to do some fishing. What happened they were excited gigging fish and leaned over to far on Bill's Airboat and it took in water. Well, we headed down the Coast and then something happened a heavy night fog come rolling in and we could not see 20 feet in front of us from the fog. Then something else happened Bill's engine quit running, that is not good as the swift currents can suck you out into the Gulf. I said let's get out of here and I threw my big rope to Bill, and I tied it on my engine frame and started pulling them back up the Coast and could not see that far ahead of me and yes, we ran over rocks, and more rocks and Allen said Dad we are taking in water I said what yes Dad and I said where at he said I don't know I said keep it bailed out. When we were coming into Aripeka it was breaking daylight. When we arrived about 30 yards from the landing my Big Ranger Aircraft Engine quit running. As we were coasting, I grabbed a paddle and kept the boat headed to the ramp. I jumped off the boat and cranked up the GMC and backed the trailer down to the water and we winched the Airboat onto it. I pulled it up on the bank and I said I'm ready to get out of here. As I was looking at the Airboat to see where we were taking in water and I puzzled me because I had 6 layers of fiberglass on the bottom and rolled it up along the sides 6 inches up. Then I found why it was leaking. It looked like someone took a knife and cut a slice into the side above where I had heavy glass. I walked around to the other side and it had a slice in it exactly across from the other side. "HOW CAN THIS BE". This true story ended up in "US AIRBOAT MAGAZINE" of Florida and it was sent all over America.

THE LORD REVEALS SOMETHING TO ME IN 1999 WITH SIGN'S, WONDERS, MIRACLES

After my Supernatural Encounter with the Lord, he revealed to me to make a Documentary about the Airboat to reach Souls for his Kingdom. We run the Airboat for 20 years at the Gulf of Mexico and the last time out one of the cylinder heads had burned a hole in it. That means make everything new again. I was blessed by a famous Airboat Race driver and engine builder as he used Aircraft engines. I filmed him all the time at the Sanctioned Airboat Races in Florida. I went to his shop and I told him I'm looking for a big rudder for my Airboat as my Uncle Ernie had one rudder on his and I want it to look just like his. He found me one and said Ken, you know this rudder is worth $ 200.00 or more. I said yes sir I'm doing a documentary for the Lord about my Airboat and he said Ken just give me $ 25.00 for it. This is the way God does business in his Kingdom when he wants something done. I filmed this man all the time. He would give a Prayer session for all the Race Drivers before the Race would start. His name was Dick and he told us how he broke his neck when he crashed his Airboat testing it. He said the Holy Ghost revealed to him what to do. He reset his neck sitting on the bank. He went to the Hospital and they X Rayed him and said it was broken and reset back in place. I always enjoyed filming him and taking photos of him as I have one in a frame at the Log Cabin here in Tn. as this photo has the wind currents and mist of water blowing by him from the Porpeller and the huge Aircraft engine with a "Supercharger" on it and it was 540 cubic inches a Lycoming Engine. The Thrust from this engine was awesome. I traveled the swamps from Wildwood, Florida to South Florida filming all the World Sanctioned Airboat Races in Florida for U S Airboat Magazine. The Lord used me to meet a lot of people and prayed for the Lord to keep them safe. The Lord opened up another door to get what he wanted accomplished. The Lord found me another Ranger Aircraft Engine we are talking about an engine built in 1942 for WW II. An automobile mechanic had one in his shop and I asked him what he was going to do with it. He said it was a spare engine for a plane and very little time on it. These Engines Cost $ 10,000 dollars. I said would you sell it to me, and he said yes. I said how much do you want for it. He said give me $ 200.00 dollars and I said yes Sir. Is God good. Now I need a New Propeller I told the Lord as he knows all things. I took our oldest grandson Zachary with me to the Races all the time. Everyone at the Races new him as he was 5 years old at the time. At one of the Races as I was filming, and a man walked up to me and said are you Ken Zifer and I said yes Sir and he said his name is Don Rowell Manager for Sensenich Propeller Co. and said I want to do something for you. And I said what is that and he said I want to build you a "Brand New Propeller" and give it to you for that big Ranger Aircraft Engine. I said Mr. Rowell can you make it solid Red in color as that is what my Uncle had on his Airboat, and he said yes. "HOW DO THESE THINGS HAPPEN", the word coincident is nowhere in the Holy Bible.

A LOUD VOICE FROM GOD FRIGHTENED ME IN 1999

In Dec. before Christmas, I went to pick up the New Propeller from "Sensenich Propeller Co. in Plant City, Florida. This is the one God Blessed us with and this Co. has been in Business since 1932 building Aircraft Propellers and now Airboat Propellers. This was the first one they built for the Big Ranger WW II Aircraft engine for an Airboat. The Big inline 6 cylinder the largest inline 6 engine WW II. The Company Head Quarters is in Lancaster PA. and Plant City, Fl., I did an interview with the Manager Don Rowell who walked up to me at one of the Sanctioned Airboat Races in Florida. He said to me are you Ken Zifer and I said yes sir as I was filming the Races for U.S. Airboat Magazine. He said I want to do something for you, and I said what is that and he said I want to build you a "NEW PROPELLER" for that huge Aircraft engine you have. I said yes sir, can you build it Red, he said yes, we can do that. At the time they wanted everyone to see the beautiful laminations of wood. We used a $ 150,000 dollar Computer Profiling Machine to build your Propeller, the only one in the world like it. This is the way "JESUS CHRSIT KINGDOM "on earth takes place, it is the Supernatural Realm. After the interview Don said he was a Pentecostal, and his Engineer was a Catholic Believer. Thank You Jesus. As I'm leaving the Company before I got off of their property something happened in the "SUPERNATURAL REALM". When I pulled up to the Stop Sign on their property I looked to the left a "LOUD VOICE" called my name, "KEN" and it was so "LOUD" it startled me and frightened me it was so "LOUD". I said to myself who in the world is hollering at me like that. I looked to me right, there was no passenger with me. Then I looked all the way around the vehicle, and no one was around. I was startled and sat there. Then God said to me in an Audible Voice again, where is the "Plan of Salvation" in your movie. I said

Lord this is not my movie this is your movie and I started to cry and I new God was involved in this to reach "SOULS" for his Kingdom. This is the way God works when he wants something done. He uses the "Insugnificant" people all the time even in the Bible. It is an "HONOR" and a "HIGH CALLING" to be in his Kingdom. The way into his Kingdom is first "Repent" of your Sins, then ask Jesus Christ to be your Savior. All through the Bible God talked to his people in an Audible Voice all the time. When the Bible states Jesus Christ is the same yesterday today and forever, he means it.

> Judges 6:25 (KJV)
>
> And it came to pass the Lord said unto him,
>
> Take thy father's young bullock, even the
>
> second bullock of seven years old, and throw
>
> down the altar of Ba'al that thy father hath,
>
> and cut down the grove that is by it:
>
> Job 38 :1-2 (KJV)
>
> 1Then the Lord answered Job out of the whirlwind,
>
> and said,
>
> 2 Who is this that darkeneth counsel by words without
>
> Knowledge?

THE EVIL DARKNESS AND THE LIGHT OF JESUS CHRIST THE PRAYER SHAWL / TALLIT BEFORE THE RACES 1993

It started out with a phone call to the President of the Sanctioned Airboat Races. Dave answered and said this to me, I have been "drastically" trying to call you as I lost your phone number Ken. Are you coming to the Races and I said yes that is why I called you to see where they will be held? He said at St. Cloud, Florida on the Lake. The next thing he said which was very strange is Ken, I need you to bring the devotion before the Races start and to the drivers. I said yes Sir. He said you know I do it all the time you know that. And then he said something is stirring in me for you to Pray for us. I said yes sir I will be there at 7:00 am sharp. On my lunch break I went home, and Cathy was headed to Tampa, Florida Hospital for a family's members baby having a heart transplant. The Prayer Shawl / Tallit that was anointed for 20 minutes by Fred and Perry Stone I put it on and "Praise and Worship" Michael W. Smith on the CD player. As I prayed in "Tongues" during my lunch break I stopped and was weeping and walked over to the phone and called Fred Stone and I left him a message, pray for me I have to bring the Devotion tomorrow at the Sanctioned Airboat Races. After work I could not find a Christian to go with me across the State to the Races. Cathy stayed up all night long praying. She is my prayer warrior. I slept peacfuly as normaly I would be tossing and turning of the excitement that would take place at the Races. I let 5:00 am and headed to Lakeland Florida to get something to eat at the Waffle House by I 4 in Lakeland. Here is where it gets interesting to say the least. When I walked in there was one man at the counter and he had a "Green" tee-shirt on, and he was from the Middle East. The waitress took my order and the only other person there was the Chef. All of a sudden, the man started a commotion with the Chef. He said you just don't know who my god is and started slapping his head with his hands and slapping his stomach and was smoking a cigarette and it sound like he had papers under his tee-shirt when he slapped his stomach. I immediately spoke out satan you stay away from me in Jesus Name. I told the Waitress I was going to move down to the other end of the Restaurant to eat. In about 5 minutes the man left the Restaurant. Was that the Darkness we have been talking about? I ate and headed to the Races and I arrived at 7:00 am and met Dave. I told him I'm going up on the hill to pray he said we will start the Races at 11: 00 am I said ok. Now it is time to do the Lord's work they had a flatbed trailer by the Lake, and I walked down by it and Dave said Ken don't go nowhere we are about to start. I said Dave these 7 feet tall speakers with Direct TV on them lined up down the track are they going to be on when I pray, he said yes. I said Lord help me. Now it's time, I climbed up on the trailer and they handed me the mic. All the drivers were standing in front of me as I looked down at them. I prayed Lord forgive us of our Sins and send your Angels around all these Race Drivers and everyone here, thank you for our President George W Bush and Lord we plead the blood of Jesus over everyone today in Jesus Name. I handed the mic to the Staff and the Races started. The one Airboat went airborne and flipped upside down. I threw my hands straight out and said Jesus, Jesus, Jesus, Jesus, Jesus, Jesus, Jesus and the speaker said the driver is ok, they flipped his boat back over and he is climbing in it and he is driving it into the pit area. Thank You Jesus. As I walked through the crowed, I said Lord what do you want me to do if something bad happens today. I heard the audio voice say run to the mic and "Bind the Spirit of Death". That is pretty heavy for a Baptist Bro. as I walked through the crowed. Everything went well the rest of the day. Now it is time for the "Bad Boy's" to race. One was a friend of mine and his last name is Hendry, and his family is the founders of Hendry County Florida along the Gulf of Mexico. He was running a Huge Aircraft Engine and he sat on the floor and 1foot from the engine in this small Airboat. He was running against an Airboat that had a full powered car Race Engine and on his Rudder was a painting of a "Dragon". I was at the finish line taking photos and when they went up to line up at the starting line, 3 children came along the shoreline in front of me to watch and I said Lord where is their parents as this was the Pit Area where all the Race Boats were. The Race started and I took the Picture of them taking off. The Thrust and Wind and Water sprayed behind them and the Aircraft engine Race Boat blew up and the other Airboat Powered with a car engine came past me and came on shore in the pit area. The race team took a four-wheeler and tied a rope to the Airboat that blew the Engine and drug it to shore, and they came by me as I took photos, the one piston was hanging out of the huge cylinder and the other piston was laying in the boat and the camshaft blew out of the motor. The drivers head was 1 foot away from the motor and he did not get a scratch. That is a "Miracle". Jesus Christ does the Miracles. They pulled the Airboat past me about 15 yards and a crowd of people went to look at the blown engine. So, I decided to walk over and take more pictures. As I started to walk over to the blown engine a "LOUD ROAR" of a Race Engine started up "WIDE OPEN" as I looked to my right it was the Airboat with the "Dragon" on the Rudders and it was headed out from land into the lake with "NO" one in the driver's seat. Then I heard a change in the sound of the roaring engine and turned and looked behind me and here the Airboat came back to shore toward me and a crowd of people. Everyone screamed and I was running, and I ran into an elderly lady with a huge pocketbook and my camara hit her pocketbook and I put my hand behind her to keep from falling on her. As this happened the Roaring Engine quit. Someone stripped the wiring on the engine to stop it. There was a man sitting in the back of the Airboat on the floor who stopped it. Thank You Jesus as a lot of people could have been killed or badly injured. This was like a dream and I told our Son Allen what happened when I arrived home and he said Dad if you would not have plead the blood of Jesus and I'm sure some of the people at the Races got in agreement with you or everyone would have been in trouble. God continues to show me things about the Evil Forces on the earth and Jesus Kingdom on earth the light. If you read the Holy Scriptures, Jesus faced the evil forces all the time, casting out Demons from people and everyone with a sickness or disease like Palsy, he called it a "Spirit of Palsy". All Believers in Jesus Christ, it's a "High Calling" and we are in his Priestly Kingdom. As we continue to a pattern of the Darkness and Light, I think this is a good time to show you what the Holy Scriptures tell us where this Evil started and what you were not told. Now what I'm going to show you I did not know as I became a Believer in Jesus Kingdom. It was not taught because it was not taught in the Seminary's and it depended on what "Denomination" you sat under. Remember when the Preacher raised up the Bible and said if you can't believe everything in this book then you need to throw it into the trash. That is a true statement it was a wakeup call for me at the age of 49 years old and sat in church all my life. As we just read true facts about what God has showed me over the years and satan does not care who he pulls down as satan and his demons work through people. In fact, as we go forward you will understand why Jesus Christ died on the cross for all the Sins on the earth and showed his disciples how these Evil Spirits attack people and he showed how to cast them out of people with his power and faith. When you become a "Believer" you have a certain amount of faith that God gives each one of us. Then it is Up To you to build that faith up.

Acts 19:16 (KJV)

16 And the man in whom the evil spirit was leaped on them, and overcame them, and prevailed against them, so that they fled out of that house naked and wounded.

SATAN AND HIS DEMONS AND NEPHILIM SPIRITS WORK THROUGH PEOPLE THE MAN IN GREEN 1998

Operation in the summer of 1998. Cathy had a major operation, and she was given the wrong medication that is deadly to her minutes before the operation. Cathy told the Nurse. When she came out of the operation on Wednesday, she had severe spasms and on Friday the Surgeon told her you need to start walking some as I'm leaving for the weekend. The only time I would leave the hospital was around 2:00 pm to go home and shower. One morning about 3:00 in the morning I walked down to the hall to get a cup of coffee and I met a man dressed in green and he had red hair and a red mustache, and I spoke to him and he would not respond and acted verry strange. On Friday evening Cathy was getting worse and around 4 :00 am I saw death in my wife Cathy, and I cried out to the Lord I need my wife Jesus help her. Cathy said she was out of pain and her Spirit was leaving her body and when I prayed, she said Ken I wish you had not as I was headed to heaven and all the pain left me. I walked down to the Nurses Station and I knew in my Spirit I could talk to her. She said how can I help you; I said my wife is dying and I'm not a Doctor, I'm a trouble shooter for the phone Company, I want to see all the charts you have on my wife Cathy Zifer. She said sure and I said Holy Ghost help me and she laid them out on the counter and as I looked at them, I saw something different. The one chart showed numbers different, and I asked why these numbers are higher here, 200 on one page and 400 on the next page and she looked and said she is "Dehydrating" I will call the doctors. They put the IV back in her and she was ok now. This took place on the "4 th Watch" when Jesus prayed the most from

"3:00 am to 6:00 am". Then later on around 11:00 am our next-door neighbor Debbi came in our room to say hi to Cathy and she said her son was in the hospital and he was down the hall from us. She went on to say something strange happened early that morning. She said she was staying in the room with her son all night and someone turned on the light in their room and she said how can I help you. The man would not say anything, and he left quickly, and Debbi said he was Red headed and had a Red mustache and he was dressed in green. When Cathy heard this, she said that same man came in her room when I went home to shower and Cathy said he picked up her Chart and looked at it and left the room and said nothing. Cathy was released from the Hospital and we asked her Surgeon who was that man and he said we have "NO ONE WORKING HERE IN GREEN" he put the word out to alert the hospital and he disappeared. Thank You Holy Ghost for guiding me and Thank You Jesus for bringing my wife back to me and for taking care of her.

John 10:10(KJV)

10 The thief cometh not, but for to steal, and to kill,

and to destroy I'm come that they might have it more

abundantly.

Ephesians 6:12(KJV)

For we wrestle not against flesh and blood, but against

Principalities, against powers, against the rulers of

darkness of this world, against spiritual wickedness

THE FIRST MIRACLE MANIFESTED IN 2003 AFTER THE SUPERNATURAL ENCOUNTER

Our grandsons were playing in the "Pal Football League". For young children ages 7 years old to 11 years old. It was the Superbowl Game, and I was on the field as always watching our grandsons and one of the Coaches was having the players do tackling drills. His Son Screamed when he got hit and I threw my hands up toward him as I was standing about 20 feet away asking the Lord to dispatch his Angels to help the child. A man walked up and said are you a Preacher and I said no I'm a Servant of the Lord and he said I'm a Pastor can I pray with you and I said sure. As I asked the Lord to heal this player. The Coach said he split his upper gum open. He will not be able to play in the game. I continued to pray. Then the Coach took his Sons mouthpiece and put it in his mount and there was not one whimper from the boy. Jesus Healed the boy's mouth. That is a "Miracle" that just manifested before our eyes in minutes. The Coaches Son played in the whole game. Thank You Jesus. Let's look at the Miracle that took place for a minute. The first thing that happened was compassion came on me, then I pointed my hands toward the boy, then I started talking to the Lord and asking him to send his Angels to help the boy. Then I asked the Lord to Heal him and then the Pastor came up and started to pray with me as the boy quit screaming. Jesus said where two or three are gathered together in my name, there am I in the midst of them. Agreement. Remember Jesus said, Thy Kingdom come, thy will be done in earth, as it is in heaven. Jesus is the Light on earth.

Matt.18: 20 (KJV)

Matt. 6: 10 9 (KJV)

THE LEGEND GOES TO THE RACES IN 2003 GOD KNOWS EVERYTHING

At a Flea Market the Lord put in our path an Artist painting and selling his artwork. I asked him if he could draw a picture of our Airboat and paint it on a shirt. He said yes and it is wild looking with the flame's coming out of the exhaust pipes and he drew me driving it and put a mustache on me. I asked him if he could draw a Fighter Plane WW II on my rudder and he said sure. He painted the big rudder solid Red and painted a WW II P 47 Fighter Plane on it Wow. And the fee was $ 100.00 it was a $ 500.00 dollar art painting. Do I need to go on about God's Power and he picks the "Insugnificant" people when he wants something done? He does it all the time in the Bible and even today. I built a new tilt trailer for the New Airboat. I'm headed to the Airboat Races with the Legend and a friend of mine who started to go with me to the Races. Big Larry was 6' 5 inches tall and weighed 235 lbs. and was rated the best lineman at the University of Ga. in the 1950's and he was a First-String Guard for the "Miami Dolphins" Pro Football Team. As we headed out early in the morning headed across the State of Florida toward Melbourne, my 1985 Jeep Cherokee Wagoneer 4 X 4 started to slow down in speed and I would give it more throttle and it did not go any faster as it dropped down to 40 mph and it did not miss or sputter. I started to pray, and I asked the Lord to send his Angels around the Jeep Wagoneer to help us get to the Races. I did not say anything to Big Larry what was going on. Within 5 minutes the speed went up to 60 mph and we drove all the way without any problems. Who does these kinds of things? When we headed down the ¼ mile fill along the Swamp, when we arrived where the Airboats were lined up all the Old Timers turned and looked at the Legend as they knew it was a design from the 1950' and 1960 Air and when we launched the Legend the people came to look at it as it is the only one in the World like it with the huge WW II Ranger Aircraft Engine on it and the one huge rudder. The crowed was somewhere around 4,000 people in the Swamp. This was one of my favorite places to film and a big day for me as the President of the Races Dave Johnson said Ken, we want you to take it down the track and don't go wide open with it. I said yes sir and me and Larry loaded up and headed down the track ½ throttle and she started to come on a plane, Larry kept telling me show them what she will do Ken. It was windy and one of the Airboat Builders from Okeechobee, Florida said he would guide us back in and when we stopped, he said Ken that motor has a good crisp sound to it which was an indication it was a Fairley new engine the Lord Blessed me with and he said you were coming up on a plane when you throttled down and I said yes and thanks. I took photos for U.S. Airboat Magazine for my friend Ron Nichols who was a very intelligent person and a fiberglass engineer. He published articles all about the engineering and fabrication of all the materials in building an Airboat and the deep things of types of metal and fiberglass and Wood Propeller Design. I shared Jesus Christ to Ron Nichols my friend. At another Race I took another Bro. in Christ with me as he had never been to the Airboat Races and when we arrived the President Dave Johnson and his wife said Ken, we need you to pray over the drivers before the race. I said ok and the Holy Ghost led me. When I was through and the races had started, one of the drivers got Air Borne with his Airboat and crashed, Jesus took care of him, Thank You Jesus. Another Race down in Okeechobee an Airboat caught fire and burned till it sunk as the driver escaped with no injuries. Another rare scene as our grandson Zachary was 5 years old at the time and he went to the Races with me as I took photos and filmed. It was in Nov. and the Races were on some private land in Okeechobee this time and in the Swamp and it was something else. Campfires up and down the Airboat track. Yes, it was cold that morning and who ever heard of having Airboat Races with campfires to stay warm in Florida, but it happened. And me and Zachary had fun. These are memory's I will not forget.

A CHOCTAW INDIAN

One of the trips to Okeechobee with Big Larry when we pulled up, I had met a Choctaw Indian at the previous Race as he was leaning on my ladder I took to film from as Big Larry was watching Zachary as I filmed. I met this Choctaw Indian and he said he was from Okeechobee and I will see you in Okeechobee at the next Race. When we pulled up that morning in Okeechobee at the track there was my friend the Choctaw Indian. When we were getting the Cameras ready, he walked up. We began to talk, and I said can I get a picture of you and he said yes. As he stood, he was shying away from his long knife on his side in a sheath. I said if you don't mind move your knife around where I get a picture of it on you, and he did. Then I said can I get a picture with you and he said yes, and I handed the camera to Big Larry. Do you see how easy it is to be kind to people and make them fill good about themselves and mention Jesus to them. He knew I worked for U.S. Airboat Magazine and I said I would like for you to tell me what the Biggest Alligator was you ever killed. He said it was a 14-footer and He said it took two boxes of 22 shorts to kill the gator. I said what else can you tell me you have accomplished, and he said he was on the "Okeechobee Search and Rescue Team" and run one of the Airboats. I asked him if he was a Christian and he said yes, his family was Catholic, and I said you know Jesus is the only way into Heaven and he said yes, he knew. I asked the Editor Ron Nichols if we could put him in the Magazine and he said sure. So, we did an article of the Choctaw Indian from Okeechobee, Florida.

WHAT IN THE WORLD IS THIS? IN THE SWAMPS OF MELBORNE

I headed to one of my famous places to film and take photos in the Swamps of Melbourne, Florida by Hwy I 95. I would leave Dade City, around 5: 30 am and get there in time to walk the long ¼ of mile of fill with Airboats up and down the Fill and with the Race Teams there. On this trip I decided to keep walking past the Airboats and see what else is along this fill and people would come from the Swamps all over to watch the Races. As I looked and said "What in the World" is this. It was a Houseboat with a huge Aircraft Engine mounted on the back deck to power the boat. Genuine Hillbilly Enginered and a one-of-a-kind Wow. They brought in a BBQ Pit that puts all of them to shame. It was at least 15 feet long and 4 feet tall and a firebox.

Luke 10:9(KJV)

And heal the sick that are therein,

And say unto them, The Kingdom of God is come nigh unto you.

WHO IS THE DARKNESS AND EVIL?

The first verse in the Bible is a good place to start. Now there are Denominations that reject what it says in the Holy Scriptures and without knowing what it says in Hebrew where it was first written you will not understand the true meaning of the word. Something to think about.

The Old Testament was written down as God told Moses what to write down just like a President of a Company would tell his secretary what to write down. The New Testament was inspired by God through men. The first verse in Genesis, THE FIRST BOOK OF MOSES it said in the beginning God created the heaven and the earth. The key word is "CREATED" the Rabbi's know the root Hebrew word for CREATED is made "PERFECT". God said he created the earth not in vain in Isaiah. Now we read in the next verse 2 that something happened, the earth was without form and void. What happened. We do know that God created his Angelic Angels first in Heaven before he created man out of the dust of the earth. The most "Beautiful" and "Anointed" Cherub Angel that God created in Heaven, full of "Wisdom" with "Musical Pipe's" and "Tabrets" created in him. He was the "Praise and Worship" leader in Heaven the closets Angel to God in the Heavenly Sanctuaries and his name is Lucifer and he "Defiled" the Holy Sanctuaries in Heaven with the Sin of Pride. God cast him down to the earth because of his Sin and he was in the Garden of Eden. And 1/3 of the Angels in Heaven followed Lucifer.

> Ezekiel 28: 13 – 18 (KJV)
>
> 13 Thou hast been in Eden the garden of God; every
>
> Precious stone was thy covering, the sardius, topaz,

And the diamond, the beryl, the onyx, and the jasper, the emerald, and the carbuncle, and gold: the workmanship of thy tabrets and thy pipes was prepared in thee in the day that thou was created.

14 Thou art the anointed cherub that covereth; and I have Set thee so: thou wast upon the holy mountain of God; thou hast walked up and down in the midst of the stones of fire.

15 Thou wast-perfect in thy ways from the day that thou wast created, till iniquity was found in thee.

16 By the multitude of thy merchandise-they have Filled the midst of thee with violence, and thou hast sinned: therefore, I will cast thee as profane out of the mountain of God: and I will destroy thee, O covering cherub, from the midst of the stones of fire.

17 Thine heart was lifted up because of thy beauty, thou hast corrupted thy wisdom by reason of thy brightness: I will cast thee to the ground, I will lay thee before kings, that they may behold thee.

18 Thou hast defiled thy sanctuaries by the multitude of thine iniquities, by the iniquity of thy traffick;

therefore, will I bring forth a fire from the midst of thee, it shall devour thee, and I will bring to ashes upon the earth in the sight of all them that behold thee.

Revelation 12: 9 (KJV)

9 And the great dragon was cast out, that old serpent, called the Devil, and Satan, which deceiveth the whole world: he was cast out into the earth, and his angels were cast out with him.

WHAT EVIL FORCE JOINED LUCIFER?

Most of you will not be taught this. It is very interesting to say the least what I'm going to show you what the Bible has to say about this other Evil force on the earth besides satan and his Demons. Why did God wait and destroy the earth after the fall of Adam and Eve? As we read another Evil force was created, it is called the "NEPHILIM" that is the name of the half Angel and half human that took place on the earth at Mount Hermon in Israel. The Angels that committed this Sin were called in Heaven the "Watchers" and the "Sons" of God there were 200 of them and they had names. They were God's family in Heaven that he created. They decided to come down on earth and come into the beautiful women. The book of Geneses chapter 6 talks about it and Jerimiah and Peter mentions it. There were Tribes of the Nephilim all over the Middle East even in Israel. When they die their Spirit stays on earth which is a Demonic Spirit. Do you see the Darkness on the earth and Jesus our "JEWISH RABBI" and Savior is the Light? Daniel killed one of the Nephilim called Goliath, remember Goliath had 4 brothers. During the Second Temple Day's the Jews new that the Fall of Adam and Eve brought a Sin nature to all that were borne and the Fall of the Angels that created the Nephilim a half Angel and half human is what upset God and he said he wish he had not created man. Then the Great Flood came.

Gneisses 6: 4 – 7 (KJV)

6 There were giants in the earth in those days; and

also, after that, when the sons of God came in unto

the daughters of men, and they bare children to them,

the same became mighty men which were of old, men of renown.

Jude 1: 6 – 7 (KJV)

6 And the angels which kept not their first estate, But left their own habitation, he hath reserved in Everlasting chains under darkness unto the judgment of the great day.

7 Even as Sodom and Gomorrah, and the cities about them in like manner, giving themselves over to fornication, and going after strange flesh, are set forth for an example, suffering the vengeance of eternal fire.

2 Peter 2: 3 – 5 (KJV)

3 And through covetousness shall they with feigned words Make merchandise of you: whose judgment now of a long Time lingereth not, and their damnation slumbereth not.

4 For if God spared not the angels that sinned, but cast them Down to hell, and delivered them into chains of darkness, to be reserved unto judgment;

5 And spared not the old world, but saved Noah the eighth Person, a preacher of righteousness, bringing in the flood upon the world of the ungodly;

PRAYER OF UNBELIEF BY A BELIEVER

A Bro. in Christ sent me an email one day and he said Ken pray for me as I have cancer and I will meet the surgeon tomorrow. When I read it, I said Bro. Philip email me your cell number so we can pray for you. This is Philip who made all the Signs for the Airboat Documentary for the Lord and he played the Banjo for the Lord in Praise and Worship and I would see him at the Crossroads in Lacoochee Fl. 11 miles north of us. A schoolteacher took the former Cowboy clothing store and turned it into a Praise and Worship Center on Friday and Saturday Night at the Crossroads on highway 301 and 575. To the west went to Trilby Florida and to the East went to Lacoochee Florida where the Lacoochee River flowed through the former Logging Town and this Praise and Worship Center sat across from a Beer Joint and the Telephone Co. Central Office was across from it where I worked. I would go to Praise the Lord as you know what God did to me in Praise and Worship in 1998. Bro. Philip would be there playing his Banjo for the Lord. Me and another Bro. in Jesus Christ would Sound the "SHOFAR" as the Praise Songs took us to a higher level. I called Philip and said we will pray for you as Cathy and Zachary are here in the kitchen with me. He said ok Bro. Ken. I told him all I want you to do is just get in agreement with me as I pray. When I started to pray Philip started saying if it is "God's Will". I "STOPPED" the prayer and walked outside to tell Philip that is a lie from the pits of hell, this is not God's will. I told him, Philip you are a Servant of the Lord reaching Soul's for Jesus Kingdom. It is not his will for you to suffer and die with cancer while reaching Souls for Jesus. I went back in the house and we started the Prayer Session again. Me and my Prayer Warrior Cathy and Zachary Zifer our grandson. As I started the Prayer again and started talking to Jesus and reminding him about what he said in his Holy Scriptures and I asked Jesus for forgiveness of our sins and told him Philip was a Praise and Worshiper for his Kingdom and he was reaching Souls for Jesus and he needed help as he was told he has cancer and had to meet the Surgeon tomorrow. I asked the Lord to send his Mighty Warring Angels to help Philip and we stood on Jesus Holy Scripture, we Bind and Loose that cancer away from Philip's body and we "Rebuke" that cancer away from his body in Jesus Name. I said Lord let this be a Testimony for Your Kingdom. The next day Philip emailed me and said the Surgeon stated the cancer disappeared. Thank You Jesus for your Healing Powers. Philip was taught the wrong way to pray for a healing. He knows now how to pray. No Preacher told me how to pray the way Jesus has showed me and my Babe Cathy showed me how to dispatch Jesus Angels to help people. Remember in the book of Hebrews, it said without "FAITH" it is impossible to please God.

> Hebrews 11:6 (KJV)
>
> 6 But without faith it is impossible to please him: for he that cometh to God must believe that he is, and that he is a rewarder of them that diligently seek him.
>
> Matthew 18:18 – 20 (KJV)
>
> 18 Verily I say into you, Whatsoever ye shall bind on earth shall be bound in heaven; and whatsoever ye shall loose on earth shall be loosed in heaven.
>
> 20 For where two or three are gathered together in my name, there am I in the midst of them.

THE POWER OF JESUS CHRIST AND SATAN THE LIGHT AND DARKNESS ON THE EARTH

Remember during Jesus Ministry he came to break satan and his demons. Everywhere Jesus went he delt with evil forces. Most of the disease was a Spirit of Infirmity, an evil spirit and don't forget satan tried to kill Jesus, he wanted him to jump off of the Temple in Jerusalem as it was about a 160 foot drop off. I did not learn all of this overnight. Jesus showed me how to pray for the sick, a Preacher or Evangelist did not train me how to pray. All the Preachers I was around all my life had no Supernatural Encounters with the Lord. How can you Preach about it if you never encountered it? God has placed a lot of Anointed people in my path. People that Jesus used to "Raise the Dead". One is Prophet John Scott here in Cleveland Tn. as I will explain how Jesus Kingdom works on earth. If you hang around Christian people and Preachers that do not believe everything the Bible states, you will not be able to fulfill the Power that Jesus "Commanded" his Believers to do. The Prophet Isaiah said this, if they do not speak according to the word in the bible they have "No Light" in them. We are talking about the Light of Jesus Christ and the Darkness of satan and his kingdom. Isaiah goes on to say those kinds of people end up looking unto the earth; and they behold trouble and "darkness". That is a "Power Statement" from Isaiah the Prophet.

THE KINGDOM PRIESTHOOD

As all Believers in Jesus Kingdom, we become a Priest over our family and one with boldness for Jesus Christ to reach Soul's. As the New High School Football Coach came to Dade City, Florida in 2003, the same people who want to pull down the New Coach Dale as I watched what was going on the Lord showed me a "Demonic Spirit" hovered over the Stadium. Why did good Coaches have to leave with good records? Remember the "Demonic Realm" works through people. This New Football Coach spoke with Authority, he called for all the parents who had teens at the High School for a meeting. He said Grades come first, then football and he said he would have a Study Period for one hour before football practice every day for students and have Teachers there to help them. In fact, he was so well liked one of his former players he coached in High School and went on to play College Football came to help him coach for free for one season and a Martial Artist Rudy came to help Coach Dale. Without "Boldness" Jesus can't use you. The Holy Ghost led me to go see the Coaches as they had a meeting in the Weight Room at School, and I did not know it. When I walked in with the "Holy Bible" in my hand Coach Dale got on his defensive and thought I was going to beat him up with it. I said Coach do you know what you are "FIGHTING AGAINST" here at this Stadium. That got his attention. I said I want to read something to you. I opened up the Bible to Ephesians and read what Paul said. We wrestle not against flesh and blood, but against "Powers", against the "Rulers" of "Darkness" of this world, against spiritual wickedness in high places. I said I'm coming back up here with my wife Cathy and we are going to "Anoint" this Stadium and all the Gates that let the people in with Anointing Oil from Israel and we will be praying over everything for you and your Staff Coach Dale. The Lords work started and the Coach and me and Cathy saw a change in the atmosphere as they moved forward in Wins. Now out of all the New Football Coaches that came to Dade City, Florida the Press gave Coach Dale so many Articles about his history as a Great Football Linebacker in College and what he had achieved as a High School Coach. One of the Press articles was, Dale Caparaso left Bellingham High in 2003 after winning 86 games – including four Eastern Mass. Super Bowls – in 12 seasons. This Team prior to Dale Caparaso had only three winning seasons in 35 years. The short neck thick chested former College Linebacker who the Press liked ran more Articles about him than any Pasco High Football Coach ever received. It was about the Students getting help on their grades by the Coaching Staff and Teachers before practice, this was new to the school. It was an honor to Pray for Coach Dale. Before every home game me and Cathy would Anoint the field the night before the game. I would go out on the field to meet Coach Dale and I would take action photos of the players and blow them up to an 8 X 10 and handed it to Coach Dale to give to the players. Some players never get their action photo in the News Papers. It was a Blessing to do this for the kids to build up their Spirit and Egal. Coach Dale accepted a player from another school who was not given a chance at Pasco and the Team accepted him and the big Quarter Back threw 60 yd touchdown passes for Pasco High, it was awesome to watch as I was on the Sidelines praying in the Spirit all the time and taking pictures and blessing the players. Dale won over 15 games in his first two years at Pasco High and led them to Postseason twice in four years. Years later Coach Dale went to Dixie Holland High School and turned that program around as a winning team that they had not seen in 15 consecutive losing seasons. Coach's goal of holding his players accountable to the team and their academics, broke the losing streak and they are rated high in Tampa Bay after winning the District Title after 24 years. Coach Dale Caparaso was given the Highest Award.

WHO WAS DRESSED IN WHITE IN MY HOSPITSL ROOM 2005

I had a rotator cuff tear. And our local Doctor sent me to a surgeon he used for his. Doctor Glenn was an Orthopedic Surgeon and he sent me to get an MRI in the Spring of 2005 and he gave me a resistance test and said you still have some strength in your shoulder. I asked him do you perform Arthroscopic Surgery and he said yes. He said Ken if it is only a ¼ tear that is what I will do. If it is a ¾ tear I will have to do an open Surgery on your shoulder. He said the MRI shows a complete tear. I'm optimistic as you have good strength in your shoulder. As we talked football, as Doctor Glenn was a good High School Football player in Melbourne Florida. He went on to say he would cut a small incision and go in and look. He said Ken I want you to be in a sling for a month as I do not want you to move your shoulder, I said yes Sri. Now they knew I was a diabetic on insulin. Cathy took me to the Zephyrhills Hospital early on the day of the operation. My Prayer Warrior Cathy was praying for me and other family members. My sugar was 73 when we left the house as I was concerned about it. As they prepped me, I told them check my sugar and they did, and I knew it was getting low. When they checked my sugar, they gave me a big dose of sugar water intravenously. They said it was up to 300 and they were ready to start on the procedure. The operation started around 2:15 pm and when I woke up that night something happened. When I woke up I perceived a Nurse was standing by my bed on my left side. I told the Nurse my shoulder is killing me, and the Nurse said, "YES WE KNOW" and as the Nurse walked down to the foot of my bed and I said it again my shoulder is killing me, the respond again as the Nurse walked across the foot of my bed said, "YES WE KNOW". As the Nurse walked along my right side of the bed toward me as this is the side, I had the operation on all of a suddenly passed out. When I woke up the second time there was "NO PAIN" in my shoulder. The Nurses when they checked me, they were at "AWE" and could not believe I had no pain after this "TWO AND HALF HOUR OPERATION". The hospital said Ken you can go home as this was around 3:30 pm. I called Cathy and she came and picked me up. I asked the Nurses do I need to leave in a wheelchair, and they said no you are doing just fine. Thank You Jesus. When I realized that all the Zephyrhills Hospital Staff wore "Blue", who was this in "WHITE AND BLOND HAIR" down to the shoulders? As I left the Hospital in a sling like Doctor Glenn said. I received a phone call from Doctor Glenn's Nurse two days after the operation and she said can you come over to the Office Monday as Doctor Glenn wants to see how you are doing, I said sure. I was operated only a couple of days ago. So, I headed over to see Doctor Glenn. When I walked in his office, he said how are you doing, and I said good. He said let's look and see how you are healing up. So, he started pulling the gauze bandage off my shoulder and he said, I have never seen anyone "HEAL SO QUICK". Then he said I think I'm going to pull these "STAPLES". I did not know I had staples in me. He left the room to get what he needed to pull the staples. When he left the room, I said Lord you know I do not like pain help me Lord no pain Lord when he does this. Doctor Glenn comes back in the room and pulls "NINE STANLESS STEEL STAPLES" out of my shoulder and I did "NOT FEEL ANY PAIN". Thank You Jesus. Then Doctor Glenn said Ken where are you going to take your Therapy at. I said Doctor Glenn, I can take it at the Dade City Hospital or by my local Doctors office. I said you have taken care of me very well so I'm going to take it here in Zephyrhills. He said good choice there is only two Hospitals in Florida that have a full-size swimming pool, one in Gainesville Florida Hospital and one here at the Zephyrhills Hospital. Thank You Jesus for taking care of me. How many people can say they had a "CONVERSATION" with an "ANGEL"? As I type this it drills my Mind, Heart, Soul, how Powerful God is. Me and Cathy will not put "GOD IN A BOX" as Servants of the Lord.

Hebrews 13:8 (KJV)

8 Jesus Christ the same yesterday, and to day, and for ever.

Acts 9:33-34 (KJV)

33 And there he found a certain man named Aeneas, which had kept his bed eight years, and was sick of the palsy.

34 And Peter said unto him, Aeneas, Jesus Christ maketh thee whole: arise, and make thy bed. And he arose immediately.

Acts 14:8-10 (KJV)

8 And there sat a certain man at Lystra, impotent in his feet, being a cripple from his mother's womb, who never had walked:

9 The same heard Paul speak: who stedfastly beholding him, and perceiving that he had faith to be healed, Said with a loud voice, Stand upright on thy feet. And he leaped and walked.

THE BOOK GOD'S GENERALS INSPIRED ME IN 2006

As I read how God picks the "Insugnificant" to do his work and how God used them in mighty ways. This book will show you how some fell and after they "Repented" God continued to use them to reach Souls for his Kingdom through Signs, Wonders, Miracles. It opened my heavenly eyes as it is a book how God used them. Just to mention a few, Smith Wigglesworth, Aimee Semple McPherson, Kathryn Kuhlman, William Brannon. This took place from the early 1900's up to the 1960's. When you see how the Power of the Holy Ghost functions you will understand. When I retired from the Phone Co. with 37 years' Service, I dropped by where we lived as a teenager on 3 rd. St. Dade City, Florida. I spoke to Mrs. McKendree about the Lord and she said they prayed for us all the time as we lived across the street from them. As we talked, she mentioned how she received a healing when she went to see Evangelist Kathryn Kuhlman in Tampa, Florida. She said I was sitting high in the top balcony when Kathryn said someone needs their lungs healed from the disease of Asthma up in the top balcony. She said as Kathryn prayed, she accepted the healing, and something happened. A warmouth came over her chest and the disease left her body. That is a "Miracle" that took place from a word of "Knowledge" from the Lord which is one of the "9 Gifts" of the Holy Ghost. That gift of Knowledge is not how much you know. That Gift is when the Lord downloads heavenly things to you about a person that needs a healing and what they are dealing with and you never have met them. Jesus functioned out of that Gift when he was on the earth. Evangelist William Brannon used the Gift of "Knowledge" all the time. A friend of mine in Cleveland Tn. went to see William Brannon and he said it was amazing how he would point out a person in the crowd that he never met and tell them to come up to the platform and he told them what address they lived at and the one lady he called up, he told her, people came against you because you Had a Divorce. You did nothing wrong as your husband was having an affair with another woman and would not change and come away from the sin, he was involved in. John Scott is my friend. He also said William Brannon would call out people who had other diseases and he would tell them what they were dealing with and God was healing them and they received their healing Right then. This is not the Evangelist that everyone in this town of 381 churches and over 43 million people looked up to who the Lord never used him to raise a person from the dead. William Brannon was used to heal people from all types of diseases and he was powerful in the Gift of Knowledge. Let's look at Evangelist Smith Wigglesworth. Smith accepted the Lord in a Methodist Church with his Grandmother around a wood fire stove in the church. He was born tongue tied. The Lord used Smith all the time and when he received the "Gift of Tongues" later in life the tongue-tied problem disappeared. Then the Lord used him to raise "14 people from the Dead". Aimee Semple McPherson was used by the Lord in healing people of diseases and she was brought up in the Methodist Church growing up also. This book will open your eyes and then you will realize what happened to the "CHURCHES"? It's called "Replacement Theology".

Matt. 10: 1, 7 - 8 (KJV)

1 And when he had called unto him his twelve disciples,

he gave them power against unclean spirits, to cast them

out, and to heal all manner of sickness and all manner

of disease.

7 And as ye go, preach, saying, The Kingdom of heaven

Is at hand.

8 Heal the sick, cleanse the lepers, raise the dead, cast

out devils: freely ye have received, freely give.

GODS GENERALS

In 2008 something manifested from what I read in 2006. Cathy bought me the book Gods Generals, why they Succeed and Why Some Failed by Roberts Liardon. After reading it I said Lord I want to see bones snap into place I read about your Servants you used I want to see this. Me and Cathy do not put God in a box. What did the Preacher tell me in 1998, if you cant believe everything in this book, the Bible you need to throw it in the trash. Jesus said go heal the sick, and cast out demons. What happened to Churches?? Jesus "Commanded" 500 people who were Believers in him not to leave Jerusalem Israel until they received the "Baptism" of the "Holy Ghost". Jesus said John the Baptist Baptized in water when they accepted Jesus Christ as their Savior. Jesus said you will receive "Power" after the Holy Ghost comes "Upon" you. Jesus said I have to leave. Jesus was taken up to Heaven after he said this. Only 120 Jews stayed in Jerusalem Israel to receive this Power. What Happened to the other "380" Believers as they did not receive the Power that Jesus commanded which was the "Anointing". Jesus Transferred the Anointing after that by the Power through Preaching his Holy words and by laying of hands on Believers to receive it. Saul in the Bible became a "Chosen" Vessel of Jesus and he had Ananias Lay hands on Saul so he would get "Filled" with the "Holy Ghost" and get "Healed". Read (Acts 9).

OBADIAH FRANKLIN HAS A VISION IN 2007

On Feb. 2, 2007 we were at a church service in Wildwood, Florida one evening as a friend of ours Obadiah Franklin who carry's the 100 lb. cross for the Lord was preaching there. Obadiah has been interviewed by all the Major Press even Fox News. He is different than most Preachers. When he was a Pastor in Clearwater, Florida the Lord spoke to him and said I want you to take your suit and tie off and dress in Red and build a cross out of a 4 x 4 beam of wood and paint it Red and leave the Air Condition Sanctuary and go reach "Souls" outside the church walls. Obadiah is the only one in the world to carry the cross from Bethlehem Israel to Jerusalem Israel on the deadliest day in the Middle East, on Ramadan the Muslims holy feast day. The Lord told him in 2002 to do this and reach Souls for my Kingdom. The Israeli Solders said to him you will not survive doing this. Obadiah told them I have Angels Camped around me doing the Lord's work. The Muslims in the Market Place in Jerusalem made him a special cheeseburger and gave it to him. Also he had a chance to witness to a young generation P.L.O. leader face to face in Jerusalem. At the evening service in Wildwood, while Obadiah was preaching, he stopped and changed his voice and said there is a "Storm" coming tonight. After the church service, several hours later I was called out on a trouble ticket by the phone co. to go to a tower site in Lady Lake, Florida as cell phone circuits were down. I had "Praise and Worship" on in the company van and when I pulled up to the Tower Site in Lady Lake, Florida I started testing the circuits and found cable problems. I called dispatch in Kansas and told them I needed some cable techs and kept the Praise and Worship on the radio. All of a sudden something happened, the Praise and Worship quit and a voice came on the radio and said there is a huge storm out in the Gulf of Mexico is moving toward

Lady Lake, Florida and it is moving in a circular motion and will hit in about 30 minutes. I called our dispatch in Kansas and told them about the dangerous storm coming and when the cable techs arrive, I will tell them as they were scheduled to arrive any minute. Here they came and I told them look toward the Gulf of Mexico and the storm as the lightning would strike and we could see the white clouds surround it. I said we need to leave as we are in danger. We left and in 15 minutes the storm hit. A tornado dropped down and destroyed a church and several homes and it did not touch a mobile home trailer with children in it. Later on that morning I had to go back at the site and the tornado twisted off Pine tree trunks that were over 1 feet in diameter along the highway and the State Patrol was guiding traffic around the huge trees that fell and the Tornado plowed across the State of of Florida cutting a path all the way to the East Coast of Florida. Thank You Jesus for protecting us.

> Amos 3: 7 (KJV)
>
> 7 Surely the Lord God will do nothing, but he revealeth
>
> His secret unto his servants the prophets.
>
> Psalm 32:7 (KJV)
>
> God is our refuge and strength, a very present help in
>
> Trouble.
>
> Psalm 3:3 (KJV)
>
> But thou, O Lord, art a shield for me; my glory, and
>
> The lifter up of mine head.

THE GREAT TRIP TO THE HOLY LAND 2007

On Nov. 29, 2007 me and Cathy left Tampa flying to NY. and as we waited for the direct flight to Israel it was amazing to see the Rabbi's dressed in their attire and their families get ready to head to Israel. The plane was loaded with Jews and our group of about 50 had fellowship the 10 hours of flight as we left NY around 10: 00 pm and when we arrived at Ben Gurion Airport as we grabbed our luggage and cameras as we were still working on the Documentary for the Lord to reach Souls for his Kingdom. The Holy Ghost reveals something to me as we walked out the doors of Ben Gurion there were several Tour Busses for Perry Stone and then the Holy Ghost said to me that is Gideon Shor standing over there. I told Cathy and she said how do you know; I said the Holy Ghost reveled him to me lets go. When I walked up to him, I said Bro. Gideon he said yes and I told him who we were. We loaded up on his bus and sat about 3 seats from him in the front of the bus. This man is one of the "Great Bible Scholars" of Israel and is personal friends with Benjamin Netanyahu Prime Minister of Israel who was Anointed to protect Israel. Also, Gideon is a "Messianic Jew" and was personal friends with the famous "Rabbi Getz" and they both Faught in the 1967 Israeli War. Rabbi Getz was picked to guard the Jerusalem "Western Wall" after the War. Do you see the "Favor of God" when you become a Believer in Jesus Christ which is a "High Calling" to be in his Kingdom? We stayed on the 6 th floor at the Hotel in Jerusalem by the Sea of Galilee. Galilee was always a freshwater lake not salt water. Wow what favor the Lord give us. We got up at 5: 30 am and the Jewish Chef's had a huge room to serve us. In the center of the room was a huge round table piled up with all types of fresh fruit and there was a line where the Chefs would prepare you eggs the way you wanted them to perfection and all types of Jewish bread and honey and pastries and fresh coffee and tea and all the water was in quart bottles from Italy. It was amazing to walk where Jesus walked and Ministered and Bro. Gideon would open his small Jewish Hebrew Bible and read a Holy Scripture to us and then he would tell us I'm going to take you to where this Biblical event took place. You probably want to know what it was like in Israel. The roads were all newly paved and at every traffic light hung a "Jewish Menorah" and it was very clean everywhere we went. The buildings were all made out of beautiful limestone and we went out to the farmland and they had big John Deer Tractors and the famous watering system they developed for all the fruit and vegetables. And we saw pine forest and where the "Giants / Nephilim" lived and the huge stones they used to make tables and chairs to sit on. The Holy Ghost showed me things, when we were at the Mount of Olives all the Guides would form a circle and talk and they kept looking at their watches. We were headed down the road as it was open country with fields and woods and suddenly Br. Gideon said hurry, hurry, and Cathy said what is going on and I said we pulled off the road by a bridge. As we got off the bus Gideon said hurry, hurry, and we walked along this creek that was dry and had a lot of stones and ahead of us was a huge ridge and a huge field to our right. Gideon said to us see the high ridge ahead of us, that is where the Philistines were Camped and look behind us do you see that high ridge ½ mile from us that is where the Israelites were Camped. Here is where Goliath came down to the field and this is where Davide picked the 5 stones out of the creek and killed Goliath in this field. Wow, Wow, that memory never goes away. We were the only ones that went to this site. That is God's Favor and he wants us to talk about these great things as the Darkness and the Light met in this field here in Israel. The reason David picked up 5 stones is Goliath had four more brothers and don't forget he came out of the "Nephilim Tribes" they were very intelligent creature that were half human and half Angel which were called the "Watchers" in heaven and the "Sons of God" who came down to earth at Mount Hermon in Northern Israel and came into the women and when that happened it caused God to get so upset, he said he wish he had not created man.

THE HUGE GOLDEN MENORAH IN ISRAEL IS READY FOR THE 3RD TEMPLE

While we were in Israel in 2007, we stood in front of the 2,000 lb. "Golden Menorah" which is ready to go in the 3rd Temple in Jerusalem. Let's look at something. In 2005 the "SANHEDRIM JEWISH COUNCIL" was formed in Jerusalem Israel for the first time since 70 AD when the Temple was destroyed. In 2006 the Sanhedrim Jewish Council made all the Priestly Garments and all the furniture for the 3 rd. Temple in Jerusalem. God used and Anointed President Donald Trump to Seal the Capital of Israel, Jerusalem in December 2017. No other President in US accomplished this Godly task. On the last day of the "Feast of Hanukkah" on Dec. 10, 2018 the Sanhedrim Jewish Council had a "New Altar Dedication" and "Lamb and Grain" sacrifice with all the Temple furniture and performed it live and said after the event they were ready to build the Third Temple. Me and Cathy watched the Dedication live event. Also, what is very interesting to me is there is "36 Scriptures" in the KJV Bible that tell where the Temple was located in Jerusalem. Around 2013 a Jewish Archaeologist found the Kings Press that they Anointed the King of Israel in the Temple close to the Gihon Spring south of the Southern Wall what is called the Temple Mount. The State of Israel owns the land and President Donald Trump "Sealed" the Capital of Israel "Jerusalem" in Dec. 2017. The Sanhedrim Jewish Council of Jerusalem on the last day of Hanukkah performed a Dedication for the New Altar for The "3rd Temple" and they brought all the furniture for the Temple out on the Altar and performed a "Lamb and Grain" Sacrifice. The End Times is getting closer.

I HAVE HEAVENLY UNDERSTANDING NOW

Now don't forget what God did to me in 1998 in the Supernatural Realm. Well God showed me how he put the Great Divine Healing Outpouring together. The Lord showed me live how he did it. Do not ever forget the book of Amos in the bible and Chapter 3 verse 7. In 2005 God spoke to Pastor Bob Rogers in Kansas and told him to pray for Todd Bentley every day so he wrote the name in his bible so he would not forget. Then God spoke to Pastor and Prophet Rob Deluca on March 8, 2008 and told him I'm going to pour out My Healing Powers on the earth in Lakeland, Florida and I will use Todd Bentley. Then on March 9. 2008 while I was watching Evangelist Perry Stone preach about "Dead Pentecostal Churches" in Brooksville, Florida that morning sitting there all of a sudden, he stopped and raised his right hand and index finger toward Heaven and said in a change of voice get ready, God is going to pour out his Healing Powers on the earth very soon, he will use the younger generation a person with Tattoos, Earrings, maybe Spiked Hair maybe Purple, this will not be some famous Evangelist. Do not "Rebuke" what God is going to do. Then me and Cathy were getting ready to fly to Cleveland Tn. to Perry Stones first "Ministry Mentoring School" and she had Praise and Worship on, and I said that is good Praise music as she was flipping the channels and it was on God TV channel. Well, we loaded on the plane in Tampa, Florida and went to the T.L. Lowery Building where Perry held the school for three days. The last day on April 12, 2008 something happened. Pastor Fred Stone was on the platform praying for us and Perry laid hands on us and prayed for us as there was 292 of us and when we sat down Pastor Fred Stone started "YELLING" God is pouring out his Healing Powers on the earth and it is more Powerful than the 30's, 40's, 50's and he shook and a young 21-year-old Mark

Casto ran up on the platform and grabbed the mic and said Bro. Fred the Vision God just gave you is taking place in Lakeland, Florida. I looked at Cathy and said I know what is going on now. God's Healing Powers is breaking out in Lakeland. We flew back home and after work on Monday I headed to Lakeland, Florida which was about 32 miles away. On the way I called Pastor Joe Cannon who I worked under in a Prison Ministry. I said Pastor there is a movement of God taking place, he said were at. I said Lakeland, Florida and I'm headed down there now. He said where in Lakeland and I said at Ignited Church on Hwy. 98 across from Super Walmart he said I will meet you down there. The controlling "Religious Spirits, Preachers, Evangelist, ran from God's Divine Power. My Messianic Rabbi friends brought their Congregations to see Jesus Power as over "150" people walked out of wheel chairs in two weeks. I saw Jesus Healing Powers Manifested as me and Pastor Joe watched. The Bible tells us the book of St John in the Bible, the disciples believed on Jesus, they became Believers when they saw the " Miracles " and many believed in his name, when they saw the Miracles. They became "Born Again Believers". When, When they saw the Miracles.

GOD'S DIVINE HEALING POWER 2008

This is what I asked God to show me after I read the book "God's Generals". There was 400 people waiting outside to get in. Pastor Joe showed up and we kept getting closer to the double doors. Now we were the next group to go in and when they opened the doors, they said the Fire Marshal will not let anymore in. Wow so here comes the Praise and Worship Leader Roy caring a huge TV not a flat screen. He set it up so all of us outside could see the Service. As we watched the "Praise and Worship" take place and then the Evangelist Ministering to the packed house of people. It was exciting to watch. And the second evening Pastor Joe went with me and we were able to go inside and watch. The Religious Controlling Spirits in Jesus day hated him. The same Religious Leaders today that rejected the Miracles of Jesus Christ and they are the same ones that came "Against" our President Donald Trump and they got "Barabbas" and they do not know what to do with him as they hold their "30 pieces of Silver" from the Government PPP Fund and their Church Doors went shut in 2020. They Rejected God's Warning.

THE FIRST DIVINE MIRACLE IN LAKELAND FL. 2008

It took place when cleaning up the bathrooms at 1: 00 am with no Preacher in the Sanctuary. Two College Students were sitting outside the church doors soaking in the "Anointing". When asked where they were from, they said we go to College down the road at South Eastern University in Lakeland. They were asked do you want to help us clean the church up and they said yes. So, they were asked to clean up the bathrooms. The one College Student while cleaning up felt something where he had a huge scar, and he looked and the huge "SCAR DISAPEARD"!

WHAT, WHAT, yes that is Jesus Power, the Light and he does not care how he does it. A huge man came to the movement of God and was going to kill himself from Depression and had his weapon with him. The Holy Ghost drew him to the Ignited Church where Jesus was showing up. He broke down crying and went up for prayer and that "SPIRIT of DEPRESSION" left his body and Pastor Steven the Senior Pastor saw the "Miracle" and made the Big Man head of Security as he was on the Platform a lot of times for crowd protection. I saw hundreds come out of wheelchairs for the first time in years some 18 years. They would shake under the Power of Jesus Christ as people prayed for them. I saw a Rabbi pray for a lady in a wheelchair for 20 minutes and then she stood up and people started to get excited and then the lady took a step and then another step and then another and she was "FREE" from that Infirmity of "Paralysis" remember Jesus said some of these are a Spirit that causes this Infirmity. There was "32 Pronounced Dead" by the Medical Field during this Outpouring and God used two Pastors by Divine Appointment to Raise two back alive. The other 30 were Raised from the Dead by Servants of the Lord soaking in the Anointing at the Outpouring in Lakeland and God used them to pray for those pronounced dead by the Medical Field and they came back alive. Over 150 people walked out of their wheelchairs by the Power of Jesus Christ in a two-week period. People went back to their Doctors and brought back medical reports where they were healed. A Rabbi walked in at the Lakeland, Florida Convention Center which held 8,000 people and he walked up on the platform and said to Todd Bentley that he was faced with a back and shoulder operation and all the pain left his body when he walked in. His back and shoulder were healed, and he said all you Rabbi's need to come and get some of this Anointing. At the Civic Center one night Evangelist Todd Bentley said the Lord revealed to him to pray for every person indevidually. Me and Pastor Joe stayed, and they estimated 1,000 left out of the 8,000 as it was around 10 :30 pm at night. We were the last 200 in line and I walked up to Bro. Todd he said can I anoint your "Shofar" and I said yes as he prayed for Me also. We didn't leave till about 1: 30 am. When you get around the Power of Jesus you sense it. We saw hundreds get healed even Pastors came from California to get healed. The Blind were healed, Lung Disease healed, Def were healed, the list goes on what a miraculous time watching God's Power and watch it live. Isn't it interesting that Jesus' disciples did not become "Believers" in Jesus until they saw his "Miracles" first and the people accepted Jesus after they saw the "Miracles"? This was aired around the world on the God TV station. One night at the Service in the Tent that held 10,000 people something different happened.

THE SHOFAR WAS BLOWN

An elderly lady sat behind me and Pastor Joe and she said where I go to church, we don't clap our hands and raise our hands in Service. Her name is Betty and I said you are in the Right church Service and a friend of hers came from Missouri with her. Then Betty's friend said to me will you blow the Shofar for Betty. I said to her I just don't blow it unless the Holy Ghost leads me, and the Service was getting ready to start. She said it again Betty needs something will you blow the Shofar. I said yes, I will. I sounded it three times the "Tekiah Gedolah". Then the Service started and after an hour of Praise and Worship Todd Bentley came down to our end of the platform and said someone out here needs a Miracle on your Kidney as you only have one. Come up and let Jesus heal you as he pointed in our direction. Me and Pastor Joe looked around and it was Betty as she headed up to the platform. This is the lady that where she went to church, they don't believe in raising their hands toward heaven and clapping their hands during Praise and Worship. When Betty went on the Platform when the Evangelist laid hands on her she fell in the Spirit and received her healing as she returned and shared her Miracle. From April 4, 2008 to October 2008 over "50,000 Clergy and 350,000 people" came to the Outpouring.

(2 Chronicles 5: 12 – 14)

12 Also the Levites which were the singers, all of them

Of Asaph, of Henan, of Jeduthun, with their sons and

Their brethren, being arrayed in white lined, having cymbals

And psalteries and harps, stood at the east end of the altar, and

With them an hundred and twenty priests sounding with trumpets

"Shofars".

13 It came even to pass, as the trumpeters and singers were as one, to make one sound to be heard in praising and thanking The Lord: and when they lifted up their voice with the trumpets and cymbals and instruments of music, and praised the Lord, saying, for he is good; for his mercy endureth for ever: that then the house was filled with a cloud, even the house of the Lord;

14 So that the priests could not stand to minister by reason of the cloud: for the glory of the Lord had filled the house of God.

A CONTROLLING RELIGIOUS SPIRT

The Lord has showed me over the years, the worst spirit is a "Religious Spirit" bar none and most people have no clue when that Spirit rises up. That Spirit controls the Service and does not allow the movement of the Holy Ghost take place but only his way. That Spirit can control the Preacher, it could be the "Board Members" or any person stopping the movement of the Holy Ghost. It can have a smile on its face or demands the way he thinks the Service should look like. One indicator is just look around and if there are no Signs, Wonders, Miracles, Salvation taking place something is wrong. That is a Dead Church. It all comes back to the Sr. Pastor of the house. Remember when the "Religious Leaders" never saw a demon cast out and Signs, Wonders, Miracles, take place. That is a "RELIGIOUS SPIRIT".

Mark 1: 21 (KJV)

21 And they went into Capernaum; and straightway on the sabbath day he entered into the synagogue, and taught.

22 And they were astonished at his doctrine: for he taught Them as one that had authority, and not as the scribes.

Luke 10: 16 – 17 (KJV)

16 He that heareth you heareth me; and he that despiseth you despiseth me; and he that despiseth me despiseth him that sent me.

17 And the seventy returned again with joy, saying, Lord Even the devils are subject unto us through thy name.

JESUS POWER GOES TO THE SIDELINES 2008

When you become a "Believer" your faith gets stronger as you read the Holy Scriptures and place yourself around people God has placed an "Anointing" on. It is "Tangible". As I continued to take photos of the High School Football Team at Pasco High School and prayed. When our grandson broke his leg that year as Quarter Back his Freshman year, Cathy said Ken did you Anoint the football field and I said no. She said you need to start Anointing it with Anointing Oil from Israel. Before each Friday night football game, I would walk on the field before anyone showed up and I had Cathy my prayer partner on the phone with me and in agreement as I went to the North Goal and Anointed the Goal Post and walk down the field to the South Goal asking favor for our Team Pasco High School and Anointed the field as I walked to the South Goal asking the Lord to send his Angels to protect all the players on the field in Jesus Name. Then when the game started, I would take action photos for the players and the Press. The Lord had me pray in the Spirit, the Gift of Tongues along the sidelines walking from one end of the field to the other to get good action photos for the Press and the players and asking the Lord we need your Angels on this play, we need the first down. After every game I would blow up the pictures to a 8 X 10 and hand them to the Head Coach to give to his players. Jesus funded the money for me to do this for the Teens. During this season I tore my Rotator Cuff again on a Total Jim Exercise Machine. As the season came close to an end. It was a Friday Night on Dec. 5, 2008 and Pasco was playing North Marion High School. I was on the field before anyone showed up with my Prayer Partner Cathy on the phone with me as I always started anointing the North Goal Post in the sign of the cross and pleading the blood of Jesus over the anointing oil from Israel and asking the Lord for favor for Pasco in this game. As Cathy was in agreement with me, I would head down the field toward the South Goal anointing the field with oil and asking Jesus to send his Angels to protect all the players, asking for no broken bones in the game. When I anointed the South Goal Post and ended the prayer, I would tell Cathy I'm thru and she hung up. Before I got off the field "Something Happened" in the "Supernatural Realm" the Holy Ghost revealed to Cathy, Ken needs to anoint the football. Cathy called me back and said Ken you need to anoint the football tonight. I said Babe how am I going to do that. She said three times you must anoint the football tonight for this game. Wow I said I will do it; I don't know how but I will. So I headed to the sidelines and sat on the bench near the sidelines. I started praying in the Holy Gift of Tongues. As I prayed here came a Pasco Coach holding a football and as he walked by as I did not know him as I knew most of them. I said Coach what football are you using tonight he said the one I'm holding; it is a special football for these "Play Off Games". Now the Holy Ghost kicks in. I said Coach bring that football here I want to "Anoint" it and he walked over and started holding it like a "Baby" with gentleness and leaned over with it. I took the Anointing Oil and Pleaded the Blood of Jesus over it and then took some on the tip of my finger and anointed close to the tip the sign of the cross and said in the name of the Father and Son and Holy Ghost, Lord we are asking "FAVOR" for Pasco tonight in this game, thank you Jesus. As I was praying on the sidelines and taking action photos, North Marion runs a big fullback up the middle at the North Goal and scores. When they go to kick the extra point, something happened. The "Supernatural Realm" of Jesus Christ kicks in. The football went straight up when it was kicked and came back down. WHAT, WHAT, yes that is the Power of Jesus Kingdom on earth. At half time one of Pasco's players told the Pasco Coaches and Team that Mr. Zifer anointed the football before the game as he was a Believer in Jesus Christ. North Marion fumbled the football 5 times during the game and the last drive with the score Pasco 13 and North Marion 12, they were on a drive of 80 yards and were on Pasco's 20-yard line with less than a minute to play and they fumbled the football. The game is over. Pasco Wins 13 and North Marion 12. The Headlines in the News Papers read, "A FLUKE SAND LOT KICK" cost North Marion the football game. We saw how God functions in the "SUPERNATURAL REALM". Me and Cathy do not put God in a Box. This is the Light of Jesus Christ at work. If you are not a Believer, you can pray all you want and the prayers go nowhere. This was a "Miracle and Signs and Wonders" that took place. The word coincidence is not in the bible.

Matt. 19: 26 (KJV)

26 But Jesus beheld them, and said unto them, With men

This is impossible; but with God all things are possible.

Acts 8: 13 (KJV)

Even Simon himself believed; and after being baptized,

He continued on with Philip, and as he observed signs

and great miracles taking place, he was constantly amazed.

A DEMON FLEES IN AN ATTIC IN A DOCTOR'S OFFICE 2008

A Doctor friend of ours asked me and Cathy to "Anoint" his office. So, we said yes. When God opens up a door, he expects us to go do his work as Believers. I said Doctor when do you want this done and he said Saturday will be good. He said I will call y'all. As we left Cathy said how are we going to do this. I said we will take Praise and Worship Music with us as satan hates it and the "Tallit / Prayer Shawl" and some "Anointing Oil" from Israel. He called us and said his Nurse would meet us at his Office and unlock the doors for us. We met her in the morning at the Building and I told her we need to pray first, and she said ok. I asked her are you a Christian she said I'm a Catholic. I said have you accepted Jesus Christ as your Lord and Savior and she said yes. I said let's pray. We joined hands and I asked the Lord to forgive us of our sins, and Lord we stand on your Holy Scriptures and we Bind and Loose and Rebuke any fowl spirit in this Building and we command it to leave in Jesus Name. The Nurse she had the codes to unlock the Office and we walked in and started at the other end of the building. I said Cathy how do you want to do this as I was turning on "Praise and Worship" music and I put on my "Jewish Tallit" and the Star of David and the Holy Cross. We had two bottles of Anointing Oil from Israel. Cathy said we need to Anoint every window, doorway, Computer and desk and chair, and vents and bathrooms in the building. We need to "Plead the Blood" of Jesus Christ over this Anointing Oil so we did as I said ok. Then Cathy said Ken me and the Nurse are going back toward the other end of the Building to start, I said ok. As we were doing the Lord's work anointing, in a sign of the cross in the name of the Father, Son, and Holy Ghost, with the Oil on everything and the doorways. Speaking and Commanding any Demonic Realm has to leave in the Name of Jesus Christ as we did his work. About two minutes later something happened. A loud "BAM, BAM, BOOM, BOOM" took place in the "ATTIC" as it left in a hurry. Cathy and the Nurse came running to me and the hair was standing up on the Nurses arm and I said it was a "Demon" that left the Office Building. Just continue to do the Lord's work. As we continued on Praying and Rebuking satan and his demons and Anointing everything. When we finished and getting ready to leave Cathy and the Nurse was looking for the lid for the bottle of "Anointing Oil" as it was not on the Doctors desk where they left it? We looked all over for it and it was gone, who removed that Anointing Oil Cap from the building. When we met the Doctor, Cathy said to him if any doors come open for the evil one, he will come back "Seven Times Stronger". Later on, he asked me and Cathy to Anoint another building for him that was under construction, we said yes, we will do it for you. Me and Cathy went to the Building and the Lord had us do something different this time. We took some New Bibles with us and wrapped them in plastic and zip lock bags and a shovel, and we buried them where the people that would come in the doors would walk on the word of the Lord and we Anointed and Prayed over those Bibles with Anointing Oil. We completed our mission for the Lord. The next time we saw the Doctor he said Ken and Cathy I took a Bible and buried it at the back door where I come into the Building. Amen, Amen, I said. Now I know in my spirit this Doctor was fighting an evil spirit and knew it. It is true that when a demon is removed, and you open up doors of sin, it will let him back in if you do not repent of the sin. And when he comes back, he will bring 7 more powerful demons with him. Me and Cathy have witnessed this, and it is sad, and it hurts your mind, heart, and soul. The Judge is God as he knows everything, and he knows who is dealing with evil and some people do not know how to fight evil because they are not taught. The Shepard over his flock is responsible for educating the Christians how to fight it. The Priest, Preacher, are held to a higher standard.

Matthew 12:43 – 45 (KJV)

43 When the unclean spirit is gone out of a man, He walketh through dry places, seeking rest, and findeth none.

44 Then he saith, I will return into my house from whence I came out; and when he is come, he findeth it empty, swept, and garnished.

45 Then goeth he, and taketh with himself seven other Spirits more wicked than himself, and they enter in and dwell there: and the last state of the man is worse than the first. Even so shall it be also unto this wicked generation.

Luke 10: 16 – 17 (KJV)

16 Whoever listens to you listens to me; whoever rejects me rejects him who sent me.

17 The seventy-two returned with joy and said, "Lord, even the demons submit to us in your name.

JESUS HEALING POWER WITH FAITH 2009

I said Lord I'm not going back for surgery again; I need you to heal it back. I would walk the Foot Ball Stadium stairs and talk to the Lord before any games started. The Lord led me to where the Florida Outpouring broke out in 2008, at Pastor Stephen Strader Church in Lakeland Florida, Ignited Church. I told Cathy I'm going down there to receive my healing in my shoulder. At the end of Service, they had Servants praying for the sick. I said to the Lord, I'm one of your Praise and Worshipers and I'm not able to raise my right hand and arm toward Heaven to Praise you. Help me. One of the Sister's in Christ laid hands on me and prayed for my healing and I fell in the Spirit. When I got up the pain was still there. I asked Zachary's surgeon to check my arm as Zachary was being released from his broken leg from last season's football game. The Surgeon said Ken you tore it again. Ok Doctor. Well, I went back to Pastor Straders Church two weeks later and after the Service I walked up to the healing line and a different Sister prayed for me. I reminded the Lord about everything and when she laid hands on me, I fell in the Spirit Realm again. When I got up the pain was gone, and I could raise my hand toward heaven again. Thank You Jesus for letting me Praise you and Serve you. That was a "Miracle" and a Testimony for Jesus Kingdom.

Hebrews 11: 6 (KJV)

6 But without faith it is impossible to please him: for

he is, and that he is a rewarder of them that diligently seek him.

THE NATIONAL DAY OF PRAYER & THE SHOFARS 2011 - 2013

As we know God opens doors when he wants something done, he picks "Insugnificant" people to get what he wants done. He uses Insugnificant people all through the bible. The First Baptist Church of Dade City, Florida came looking for me to blow the shofar for them on the "National Day of Prayer" at the towns square. When they approached me, I said it would be an honor to do that. The Rabbi they used had to leave his Congregation to come across the County to do it. I asked one request and that was to give me a few minutes to explain to the crowed of people what it represented as I did not what the Priest and Preachers and some of the Christians to look around and say what is that about and what is that instrument? I also asked them if our Son and another Bro. could blow the shofars with me and they said sure. God knows all things as I let the Holy Ghost guide me. The day of the event they told me Bro. Ken you will be the first speaker to open the National Day of Prayer with the shofar. This will be an honor to do this for you I said. When the day arrived, I told the Holy Ghost to speak through me. Pastor Joe Cannon was standing by me and our Son Allen and Bro. Joe. The Lord had me open up with a word of prayer as I addressed, Rabbi's, Priest, Preachers, and Brothers and Sisters in Christ, forgive us of our sins Lord and Holy Ghost speak through me in Jesus Name. The Lord had me explain about the Shofar. The word trumpet in Hebrew is shofar unless it is a Golden Trumpet or Silver Trumpet. The first place it is mentioned in the bible is in the book of Exodus when God came out of the Heavens to meet Moses. When God showed up there was thunders and lightnings, and a thick cloud and the sound of the shofar and fire and smoke. The shofar is an instrument for Praise and Worship and a Weapon of God's. The first instrument the Psalmist mentions in Praising Jesus Christ is the Shofar.

When we sounded the Shofars, the Southern Baptist turned loose "White Doves", over our heads as we did not know they were going to do this. What a moment not to forget. We blew the major sounds of the shofar, Tekiah, Shevarim, Teruah, Tekiah Gedolah as the crowed watched in this Southern Town in Florida. Then the Preachers came forward to bring a word of prayer for our Nation with the Parents and children and College Students. In 2012 the Lord had me mention that our President in 2008 signed an Executive Order for "2 Billion" for Abortion around the world. After all the Clergy spoke the First Baptist Church Youth group sang Praise and Worship songs and when they sang the song "OUR GOD IS GREATER" and something happened. My Spirit raised up in me and I stood up while the song was played and not far from the podium and raised my hands toward heaven and then raised the shofar and sounded the "Tekiah Gedolah" three long blasts, the Great long Blast. The Catholics came running to me and said they never saw anything like this before. I said a Revival started to break out, did you see the Southern Baptist Youth, they raised their hands towards heaven in Praise and Worship. I told the Sr. Pastor at the First Baptist Church there is your Praise and Worship Leader, Vickey Balogh. Behind the scenes they did not want Bro. Ken to talk about the deep hidden "Mysteries" in the bible. Something they were not aware of as I explained that the "FEAST OF TRUMPETS" when the Shofars are blown 100 times in Israel, that day was the only day during Jesus time that they did not know the day or hour for that Feast. The High Priest at the Temple in Jerusalem would send out his Priest to search the heavens day and night looking for the little sliver of the moon. When they saw it, they would run back to Jerusalem at the Temple and tell the "Sanhedrim Jewish Council" and they would tell the High Priest and he would stand in the Temple with his hands towards heaven and would say it has begun. Also, the Hebraic Holy Scriptures tell us on that Feast Day they blow the Shofar's 100 times as they prepare for the return of Jesus Christ as Paul told us when we here the "Trumpet / Shofar" of God we will be caught up. That is the Rapture Paul is talking about. He also states again I shew you a "Mystery" in the twinkling of an eye at the "Last Trump" the sound of the Shofar is the "Tekiah Gedolah" the long, long sound of the Shofar. Isn't it interesting that God never put the sound of the Shofar in Lucifer? The Rabbis will tell you the sound of the Shofar makes satan and his demons think it is God's voice. God came out of the heavens with the sound of the Shofar and the people trembled, the sound God used was a long, long, sound that is the Tekiah Gedolah sound the "Last Trump". The Hebrew writings tell how the Shofar was sounded at every Feast at the Temple in Jerusalem. The Shofar changes the atmosphere when sounded.

1 Thessalonians 4:16 (KJV)

16 For the Lord himself shall descend from heaven with

A shout, with the voice of the archangel, and with the

trump of God: and the dead in Christ shall rise first:

1 Corinthians 15:51-52 (KJV)

51 Behold, I shew you a mystery; We shall not all sleep, but we shall all be changed,

52 In a moment, in the twinkling of an eye, at the last trump: for the trumpet shall

sound, and the dead shall be raised incorruptible, and we shall be changed.

A HUGE BBQ PIT TO REACH SOULS 2014

God sees all things and knows all things. In 1991 the Holy Ghost showed me how to build an open "BBQ Pit" the first one in Pasco County, Florida to BBQ a whole 210 lb. hog for our Son's Wedding. I used a solid ¾ inch steel shaft and welded three stainless steel pins vertical on it so the pins would hold the hog on the steel shaft. I built pullies off the end of the shaft and geared it down to a slow turning motion with an electric motor. It stood 4 ½ feet off the ground. We went to the hog farm and I picked out a 210 lb. hog and the farm had it ready to load up and we headed home with it and used the crane I built to pick up engines to lift the hog and skin it and we put it on ice while I finished up welding an expanded metal table to go under the solid bar of steel hanging the hog on. We headed to Lake Iola and built a big pit with split wood two truckloads that Johnnie Blommel brought for us and Uncle Ernie Petters and Bill Jones and Veral Harbison came to help me with everything but the kitchen sink. We dug down a foot under the pit and placed three bags of charcoal and then the firewood on top and lit it at 7:00 pm in July and sat around the campfire drinking coffee and tea and talking about the hunting trips and fishing trips.

Doug Sanders a friend of mine was the first one to start filming God's Project for us. He brought his Professional Wisdom and Camera Equipment to film the Campfire scene and did interviews with us for the documentary. Uncle Ernie Petters was one of the Great outdoorsmen in Florida he was the first to do the Cowboy scene with Marlboro Cigarettes and he was well known in Okeechobee Florida Rodeo events. As we talked about some great outdoor adventures bro. Jones told how efficient Uncle Ernie's Airboat was and Ernie told us how the Game Commission let him use their fish net. One day my Dad Tony could not find any bait fish the wild shiners at the Bait House in town. So, Uncle Ernie said let your boys go with me and I will get you some shiners to fish with. We loaded up and Ernie had most of the keys to all the pastures in Pasco County. We went out in this pasture and there were some ponds out in the area. We started to sane the pond and wow we caught all kinds of freshwater fish. We caught two 5-gallon buckets of shiners for Dad. We had a picture of one of Uncle Ernie's duck hunting trips. The 1957 chevy truck was so loaded down with ducks, they were falling off the bed of the truck. He used his Airboat and Browning Shot Guns to get the ducks. Ernie was a Giant of a man in that day. At 6' 3" and 230 lbs. a Swedish and German descent he had no fat he was a gentle giant of a man. Everyone loved Uncle Ernie. Rabbit hunting, we would go with him and come back with 10 – 20 rabbits. Hunting with him one time I saw him catch bare handed a wild boar razer back hog. He killed 60 deer in one season with permission of the Florida Game Commission in South Florida. He would take the Governor of Florida out fishing on the Great Airboat. I shared the plan of Salvation with him, and Obadiah Franklin ministered to him in the hospital when he passed away. He was so proud of the News Paper Article about the rebirth of his Airboat the Legend the only one in the World like it, with the Largest WW II Aircraft engine on it and a Tractor Propeller. This Camp scene was posted in the Local News Paper in Dade City, Florida. The campfire stayed all night with flames of fire, and it took 18 hours to BBQ the 210 lb. hog and we feed all the High School Football Coaches at Pasco High School. The Coaches that coached our Son Allen as he was headed on a College Football Scholarship at Tusculum University Tn. as a first-string Middle Linebacker after his wedding. All the family and friends were there for the celebration at the Lake. The BBQ Pit continued to reach Souls for God's Kingdom. Thank You Jesu

GOD USES LEXI AND CATHY TO SAVE MY LIFE 2013

One morning around 9:00 am I was getting ready to go into Dade City to get a cup of coffee and eat breakfast and study the Holy Scriptures. I checked my sugar and took some insulin. When I was through shaving and I grabbed my toothbrush, I did not know anything else as I passed out and fell into the shower Curtin and tub. When I woke up, I tried to get out of the tub and my muscles would not get me out. I knew I was in trouble as I talked to Jesus it was a slurred speech and I knew my sugar had dropped. I was only about 15 feet from a floor cabinet with sugar in it. I could not get to it. I was dying and I knew it. I was so desperate to live I grabbed the metal shower Curtin Rod with my teeth and hands and tried to pull myself up out of the tub. My muscles would not let me. I said Lord why is this happening to me? I said, "JESUS HELP ME". As I did not know, Jesus used Lexi our Blonde Shih Tzu dog as she ran upstairs. She was never allowed upstairs and she pawed on the bed to warn Cathy I was in trouble. Cathy woke up and Lexi ran to the bedroom door and looked back at Cathy. As Cathy said what happened, Lexi ran over to the bed again and pawed on the side of the bed and ran to the door again. Then Cathy heard me, and she knew I was in trouble. She tried to give me some orange juice and called 911. When they arrived, they fed me intravenous a sugar solution to bring me back. The Medics said my sugar was 20 so it was lower than that as it was 11:00 am when they tested me. Jesus used Lexi many other times when satan tried to take me out. Jesus it is painful for me to talk about Lexi as we had to put her to sleep because of two bad discs in her back and she was only 6 years old. We made sure she was not in any pain as I asked Cathy can't the Vets put her to sleep like for surgery and then put her to sleep so she doesn't feel anything and no discomfort. Cathy said yes and our Vet in TN. helped us with that procedure. It hurts me to talk about her. We had a Soul Tie with Lexi. I walked her on Lee Campus every day and before work at times. A lot of Professors saw me, and Cathy and Lexi and I would carry Lexi into some of the Professors Offices. I don't know how to explain the bond we had with Lexi. I would kiss her all the time and we took care of her like a person. She was our family when we moved to Cleveland Tn. in 2014. She would wait for me looking out the window waiting for me to get off work. It hurts me to type this. It was such a shock for me and Cathy when she passed away, I could not function properly and could not work on our Log Cabin anymore on the inside. Our grandson Zachary who God placed in a High Position in DC called us one night as he was getting ready to Graduate from an Agency as they picked him and 23 others out of 150,000 people and assigned him to --------- in DC. He said Pawpaw do you Owe anything on your Cabin or Land, and I said no. He said take your keys and lock up the Log Cabin and you and Nana come up here I don't have any family up here it is me and my wife Olivia and our Son who was 2 years old and our Great-grandson and we had not seen him. So, we made another transition. Zachary said in his conversation, Pawpaw wherever you go God is going to use you. When Zachary reached out to us it took the depression off of me to where I could function. Thank You Jesus for using Zachary and Olivia to help us. On October 31, 2018 I flew up to Maryland for Zachary's Graduation as on this secluded land, only the President and his Staff is allowed on it. They only allowed 6 family members for the Graduation and Cathy stayed with her Sister at the Cabin. Her Sister Karen headed back home to be with her family as she was helping us finish the Log Cabin. As I'm typing this, I get really silent and still as my mind and flesh think of Lexi. I used to train hunting dogs and had dogs for hunting for many years. I never had a relationship with a dog like I did Lexi. Jesus used her and she knew if my sugar started to drop. Jesus tells us in his Holy Scriptures the benefits he has for his Believers in heaven. I will explain it to you for those who had a pet they loved. Dr. Graham stated that Believers when they go to heaven, they will see their pets. His friend Dr. Van Impe proved in the Holy Scriptures and went back 100 years to some Theologians who wrote about animals and pets in heaven. I want you to think about something that entered my mind after Lexi left us on Sept. 11, 2018. Remember when God took Elijah to heaven as he never died. When Elijah and Elisha who Elijah trained as they were walking and talking, behold, there appeared a chariot of fire, and horses of fire, and Elijah went up in the chariot with a team of horses and a whirlwind to heaven. You mean there is horses in heaven and other animals, yes, the Holy Scriptures tell us. Beast is Animals. All Believers will be with their loved pets in heaven that is one of many benefits we receive. Jesus Loves his animals, he created them for us. The animals Praise and Worship Jesus. This is the unknown realm where Jesus lives and Reigns.

Revelation 5:11 (KJV)

11 And I beheld, and I heard the voice of many angels round About the throne and the beasts and the elders: and the number of them was ten thousand times ten thousand, and thousands of thousands;

12 Saying with a loud voice, Worthy is the lamb that was slain To receive power, and riches, and wisdom, and strength, and honour, and glory, and blessings.

DARKNESS COMES TO THE NATIONAL DAY OF PRAYER 2014

The Southern Baptist Church brings in a New Pastor and as I picked up the bulletin and read it they stated the National Day of Prayer for 2014 would start at 1: 30 pm not at 6: 00 pm. That ment it was set up for the "RELIGIOUS LEADERS" and the "Elite", the children and parents and working people could not pray for our Nation. Do you see how satan and his demons work through people? He does not care if you are a Preacher or not. Less than half of the people showed up for the event at the town square. NO REVIVAL BREAKING OUT. What did Jesus say about the Demonic Realm? Everywhere he went he faced demons and he trained 70 how to cast them out of people and have discernment of the evil forces. Let's look at something, satan tried to kill Jesus, he tempted him three times and the last time he wanted Jesus to jump off of the Pinnacle on top of the Temple in Jerusalem which was about 160 foot drop off. This was not a Preacher satan was dealing with it was the creator of the earth Jesus Christ who created everything in it.

> Matt. 4: 5 (KJV)
>
> 5 "Then the devil taketh him up into the holy city,
>
> and setteth him on a pinnacle of the temple,"
>
> 6 And saith unto him, if thou be the Son of God,
>
> Cast thyself down: for it is written, He shall give
>
> His angels charge concerning thee up, lest at any
>
> Time, thou dash thou foot against a stone.

TRANSISTION TO TN MORE MIRACLES MANAFEST 2014

On June 13, 2014 at 3:30 pm me and Cathy headed to TN. It looked like a Train. The U-haul truck was a 29-footer, and I was pulling my 1990 Jeep Wrangler on a toe dolly and connected to the Jeep was a trailer with the Big BBQ Pit on it and a crane to lift the 8' long lid. The total length was 79 feet long. When we arrived on Interstate 75 and headed North, truck drivers would pass us and give us the thumbs up sign, as we had a Sign on the Jeep, headed to Cleveland TN. When we came into Atlanta, Ga. about 2:00 am, Cathy said Ken why is the car behind us giving us the bright lights. As it started to rain some and when I looked as I went through a sweeping curve our BBQ Pit trailer was in the other lane. Lord help us. When we arrived in Cleveland TN. around 9:30 am I pulled up to the Howard Johnson Hotel and Cathy could not get out of the truck for her back was in pain as she had back surgery from a blown disc from years prior. She had to wait 30 minutes before she could get out of the truck. I was unhooking the Jeep and she was in a lot of pain as we entered our room. I felt stranded and thought I was going to have to call 911 for Cathy. We prayed and the Lord took care of Cathy she could get out of bed later and the Ministry did not return calls as they knew we were coming, and they were going to unload the truck for us. But it was Father's Day weekend. This is how the Lord helped us get the truck unloaded. The Lord sent a "Rabbi and Three Baptist" to unload the truck for us the next day. I will never forget the Rabbi and Sister Nelms and her teen age Son and his friend. We were strangers to the new town. Rabbi David is a friend of ours and is very intelligent person and he is a "Messianic Rabbi". We picked our Insurance Agent, and his name is Jim. He helped us tremendously and found a house to rent next to Lee University. This is how God took care of me and Cathy. The owner is Bro.

Eldrin Boehmer, and his Dad was one of the men to help start the Oldest Pentecostal Churches in North America. When his Dad went to California to see his Sister, he was walking down a street and he heard someone speak in German. He walked over to the Church where he heard someone speaking in German and the Preacher said to him how can I help you and Bro. Boehmer said I heard someone speak in German. The Preacher said we don't have anyone here that speaks German. There were some people speaking in "Tongues" and Bro. Boehmer said it was fluent German. Bro. Boehmer received the Gift of Tongues while he was there and came back to Cleveland Tn. and helped start the Oldest Pentecostal Church in North America and it is the Church of God North Cleveland Tn. and Dr. Billy Graham went to College here before it became Lee University. We are renting three houses from the church as we are plowing to build a Log Cabin. God works and functions in the Supernatural Realm. The Holy Scripture reveals that God said build me a house out of "Cedar". The Holy Ghost guided us to a Log dealer in Oregon and the Price on Cedar Logs was $ 30,000 for our home. God's price was $ 13,500 from the Log Dealer in Oregon. The first Miracle in Cleveland Tn as the Lord had me pray for the tractor driver clearing the land that a former "Muslim" found for us as we searched for 6 months for land that would meet our budget. One morning at the Cabin, I asked the tractor driver how he was doing, and he said his wife had cancer. He was a Believer and I said I'm going to pray for your wife. Just get in agreement with me and he said sure. His wife went back to the Doctors and the cancer disappeared. That is a Miracle by Jesus Christ. God will put people in your path to minister to. All Believers are Priest in Jesus Kingdom. As we supported Perry's Ministry, we saw Signs, Wonders, Miracles, take place. In 2015 I asked Pastor Mark to pray for my Dad who was close to passing away. He led the prayer with our prayer team, and he asked the Lord for a smooth transition to heaven for my Dad. That did happen. When I called my Dad after that prayer, he said Ken I Love You and I Love Jesus. What a transformation he went through and he passed away peacefully, thank you Jesus. During Praise and Worship, I would us a Banner and Shofar to Praise the Lord. As you know what Jesus did to me in Praise and Worship in 1998. That "Supernatural Encounter" never goes away it changed me forever. No Preacher could tell me what I encountered, they could tell me about people accepting Jesus Christ and very few could mention a Miracle taking place. We supported and helped Perry Stones Ministry in Cleveland Tn. When I went to the Service, I did not go looking for Tom, Dick, and Harry. I went looking for Yeshua / Jesus at the Altar in Praise and Worship. I would pray in tongues and raise my Spirit up to a higher level and then bask in the Supernatural Realm with the Lord. Yes, the Numbness, Weightiness, Sensation would come on me as I basked in Jesus Presence during Praise and Worship. At the Main Conferences I was on the Prayer Team and Prayed for people at the Altar. It was a different setting than the "Divine" appointments I was familiar with. The Fire Tunnels were Powerful. That is when the Believers on the Prayer Team line up in two rows facing each other and about ten feet apart and we would start praying and the Teens and Adults would walk through and we would lay hands on them and some would encounter the Holy Ghost and start speaking in Tongues and a lot of them would fall in the Spirit. That is when a person falls in the Presence of the Holy Ghost and encounters the Power of Jesus Christ and lays there in his Presence. It was awesome to minister to the people and watch God's power come on them. Then the Fall Fest came to Perry Stones Ministry and the Big BBQ Pit that the Lord had me build, the only one in the World like it as I had to build a crane for it to lift the 240 lb. lid that was 8 feet lang. A friend of ours who was a "Five Star Jewish Chef" and a Minister who we lived by at Lee University helped me cook at the event. We cooked for Pam Stone some Boston Butts for the Hebrew Café at Perry's Ministry. It normaly takes 9 ½ hours to cook them. The Chef David said Ken I need 400 degrees; he was used to cooking in an elaborate Kitchen as a 5 Star Chef is used to. I said Bro. David hold on as we were cooking with logs of wood. Let me set the draft and I will get it at

400 for you. The Boston Butts were done in 4 ½ hours with the Big BBQ Pit the Holy Ghost told me how to build to do Jesus Kingdom work. On this October Feast in 2014 I was also there to make some pocket change to help us with building the Log Cabin for our home. The next day me and David the Jewish Chef were there early getting ready for the crowd after the Conference, and I had the fire ready with plenty of logs. This is what I love to do is cook for the people and make them happy. David said Ken you collect the money from the people, and I will do the cooking as this is your Project. The line was over 200 people long who was placing their orders for ¼ pound all beef hotdogs and hamburgers with all the fixings. We worked hard and had fun. Bro. David was a true 5 Star Chef, and it was a Blessing to know him and work with him. I met a lot of Brothers and Sisters Serving them food at this event. The Hot Dogs I had could not be purchased at any local Market. As the flames of fire and glowing wood coals burned, we had fun. After the event I handed Bro. David $ 500.00 and he did not know what to say as his electric bill was $ 300.00 and he said Ken thanks several times to me. Thank You Jesus for putting David the Jewish Chef in my path. He passed away two years later as he moved to Knoxville, Tn to Serve the Lord up there. The Ministry asked me to cook 200 hamburgers for their first Baptism and a young Bro. in Christ from the Jungles of Africa came to help me and yes, he kept me out of trouble making sure the flames of fire didn't burn the hamburgers and made sure they were done as I had my hands full loading the Pit with firewood and setting the air vents to keep everything going to Serve the Body of Christ. His name is Emanual, and he was a blessing to say the least. God is good all the time when you get around people who love the Lord. To give you a picture of the BBQ Pit, it is 14 feet long and stands about 5 feet tall. The crane is 9 feet tall to lift the 8 foot long lid. The Holy Ghost said go reach Souls for my Kingdom with this BBQ Pit and we had a lot of fun and yes, it is hard work. The 200 lb. whole hog cookout that was to take place never happened as things changed quickly.

TWO CAVATIES DISAPEAR 2015

Before we left Florida to head to Tn. a Bro. in Christ Ronnie Pitts said Ken, we have a traveling Dentistry coming to the First Baptist Church in Lachoochee. It's free. The Dentist, X-rayed my teeth and I had 3 cavities and he said I will fix the worst one. I said thanks Doctor. I prayed for no pain and that is what I received. The Dentist said now Ken you have two cavities left don't forget it. The Shofar was blown for the first time in this 100-year-old church in Lachoochee. Bro. Ronnie invited me on a Wednesday night to sound the Shofar in this Southern Baptist Church and it was an honor to do that for the Lord. I blessed Bro. Ronnie with a Shofar from Israel and he passed away to heaven shortly after. Now after building the "BBQ PIT" to reach Souls for Jesus Kingdom, me and Cathy and Lexi headed to Cleveland TN on June 13, 2014. In 2015 I found a Dentist in Cleveland that cleans teeth with no pain. When I filled out the Dentist Form, I stated I had two cavities and needed my teeth cleaned and turned in the form. When I went back for X-rays and then the Doctor Chandler came back to look at my teeth and he was very gentle, and he said you do "NOT" have any cavities. I spoke up and said on my Dental Form I stated I have two cavities as they X-rayed my teeth before we left Florida about 6 months ago. Dr. Chandler said Ken you have "NO CAVITIES" and you have 3 broken teeth and I have never seen this before, there is "NO CAVITIES" trying to form on your teeth. After he checked my teeth, his dental hygienist cleaned my teeth. She was very gentle as she would clean for a minute and rinse and then start cleaning again. This was a first for me. Thank You Jesus for taking care of me and Cathy. Then Cathy's cap on her tooth came off in 2017. I said to her what Dentist do you want to use, she said Dr. Beard. We were new to them, so I took Cathy, and the Father and Son Team took Cathy in and Ken Beard placed the cap back on while I was talking about the Lord at the front Desk. When they were through fixing

Cathy's tooth, the receptionist said Ken because you are a Veteran give us a call on Veterans day at 7:00 am and we will take care of you. Cathy's fee was taken care of by the Lord and his Servants the two Dentist. Thank You Jesus. Then two Miracles took place at Petco on Paul Huff by Divine Appointment. The one girl told me about her boyfriend was faced with a second surgery on his broken ankle. I told her lets pray for him, just get in agreement with me as I talk to the Lord and quote a Scripture to him. When I took Lexi back, she said Ken my boyfriend his ankle healed back, and the surgeons were amazed. The other groomer told me her 14-month-old baby was diagnosed with diabetes. I told her lets pray about it and Rebuke it away from her, just get in agreement with me and I said Lord forgive us of our sins, and this is your baby Lord and remove that diabetes from her Lord. Two weeks later the Doctors said she is clear of Diabetes. About a year later I saw her at Walmart shoping and I asked her how the baby was doing and she said Ken she has no diabetes and is doing great. I told her Jesus is the healer she agreed. Thank You Jesus for using me in your Kingdom.

JESUS SHOWS UP IN WALMART CLEVELAND TN. 2016

The Ministry takes a major turn quickly. Now during this Transition taking place the Lord opened up a door for me to finish the Log Cabin. Walmart Super Center on Keith St. in Cleveland Tn. hired me as a Security / Host. I will never forget as I hired on Aug. 31, 2016. God wants to use all of his Believers to reach Souls for his Kingdom wherever you are and don't forget it. Souls are outside of the Church Walls. Look where Jesus Ministered. He did not spend a lot of time Ministering in Jerusalem Israel where most of the people were. His Ministry was 80 % around the Sea of Galilee which is a Fresh Water Lake. The first day at work as I walked across the parking lot which was 150 yards away, I said Lord thank you for the Job and "USE ME" Lord any way you want. Jesus Christ knows your heart and he uses the "Insugnificant" people all through the bible when he wants something done. About two weeks later one Saturday morning as I was walking to the Grocery doors from the parking lot as I always talk to Jesus on the way and to clock in at 7 :00 am. I spotted my boss at the doors and he waved at me from a distance and was waiting on me. As I walked up to Keith, he entered the store and me behind him. I said to him well boss how are you doing and he stopped and turned and looked down at me, as Keith is 6 foot 5 inches tall. He said well you asked so I'm going to tell you. My heart rate is 33 and I need a "Pacemaker". Something happened to me wright then. Boldness raised up in my Spirit, I raised my right hand and index finger towards heaven, and I looked up to heaven and said I'm going to "Rebuke" that Pacemaker away from you. Then Keith said I believe in prayer and then he started to walk to the back of the store, and he took a right past the produce section to head to our break room and his office to clock in. He stopped and when he did the Power of the Holy Ghost Manifested. I looked up at him and said Keith I'm going to pray for you. I do not want you to say anything, just get in agreement with me as I'm going to talk to Jesus. I said Lord forgive us of our sins, and Keith needs your help. I said Jesus I'm going to remind you what you said. In Matthew 18: 18 you said whatever we bind and loose on earth is bound and loosed in heaven. This is one of your "Mysteries", we bind and loose that pacemaker away from Keith's body and Lord restore his heart and let this be a "Testimony" for your Kingdom Jesus. Something else happened to me. My "Faith" level raised up so high in my Spirit, I said Keith get ready God is going to heal you and you will come to me with a testimony so get ready. Wow it was a now word with power. This does not happen to me all the time. A couple days later here comes my boss Keith walking toward me from the grocery section as my post that morning was at the Pharmacy doors. As he got closer to me about 20 feet from me, he said the Doctors, and when I heard Doctors, I yelled and raised my hands straight towards heaven and said give me the "Testimony" as I get excited for the Lord and I did not care if any people walking in or out of the store saw me. Keith said the Doctors said something happened. They said my heart rate was normal and they checked my heart and said it is normal. I raised my voice and said that is a "Miracle" Keith and don't you ever forget what the Lord did for you, and he said Ken I will never forget it. Then I find out his Dad is a Preacher in Cleveland Tn. and I met him one day in the Store and they look like twins and he is a very kind Preacher and he told me he went to Israel also like me and Cathy. Jesus is more "Powerful" than people think. Don't forget something, in the town of Cleveland Tn. there are "381 Churches" Preaching the Gospel of Jesus Christ. I want to educate you about what an Evangelist friend of mine Bro. Todd told the Body of Christ. When you become a Believer in Jesus Christ the Lord gives you a certain amount of faith. Then when you read the Holy Scriptures, you will get more faith in your mind, heart, soul. Then when God wants to heal someone, he will download you, "Supernatural Faith" when he wants a Miracle to take place. Jesus functions out of the "Supernatural Realm" and that is where he wants us to function out of to bring his Kingdom on earth. Let's look at what happened that Saturday morning. First, I was talking to Jesus when I got out of my Jeep and the walk to the doors are about 150 yards away. Second a darkness came over Keith as he was facing heart issues. Third thing that happened was "Boldness" rose in me. Fourth, it was a "Divine Appointment" for me to pray for Keith. Fifth, my Faith rose so high I knew Jesus was going to heal him. Sixth I shouted and raised my hands towards heaven in joy and shouted don't forget what God did for you even in front of the public. I'm a Servant of the Lord, I'm in his "Priesthood" as a Believer I'm in "THE KINGDOM PRIESTHOOD" for Jesus Christ, it is a "High Calling" to be in his Kingdom. You may want to read the book Dr. Michael K. Lake wrote about last summer. The Kingdom Priesthood: Preparing and Equipping the Remnant Priesthood for the Last Days. Dr. Michael K. Lake is a Chancellor and holds Doctorates in Theology and Religious Education and has 35 lexicon languages and knows Hebrew to research the Hebraic Scriptures and the King James Holy Scriptures.

Hebrew 11: 6 (KJV)

6 But without faith it is impossible to please him:

For he that cometh to God must believe that he is,

And that he is a rewarder of them that diligently seek him.

THE SECOND MIRACLE IN SUPER WALMART CLEVELAND TN. 2016

On a Friday night at my post at the Pharmacy doors, my boss was headed home, and I told Keith my time needed to be corrected from my lunch break. He said Ken Cathy our Personnel Manager is in her office she will fix it for you. This was around 9 :00 pm when I went to see her. When I walked in her office, she was sitting with some of our personnel at the row of computers. I said Cathy and she said Ken I will be with you in a minute. So, I sat down by the door and one of the girls said to Cathy what are you going to do with your foot, you can't walk. And Cathy said I just came back from the Walk In Clinic and they want $ 100.00 to ex ray my foot and fix it. I noticed she had her shoe off her right foot. I knew she was raising her grandchildren and money was a concern for her. When she stood up, she drug her foot and leg to her desk and she sat down and said Ken how can I help you. I walked over and told her about my time sheet. She said Ken it won't take me a minute to fix it for you. I knelt down on one knee by her desk as she fixed the problem. Then something happened in the "Supernatural Realm" I said Cathy you just fixed my problem; can I fix your problem and pray for your foot and she said please. I said Cathy I do not want you to say anything, just get in agreement with me. I spoke to Jesus and told him you know everything about Cathy, and she needs your help. I said Lord forgive us of our sins, and we Bind and Loose that infirmity away from Cathy's foot and we Rebuke it away from her foot in Jesus Name and Lord, let this be a Testimony for your Kingdom. I left the room as there were four other employees in the room. When I do the Lord's work, I don't care how many people are watching. I went back out on the floor at my post and then it was time to log out at 10 :00 pm. So, I did and then I decided to buy a few groceries to take home. As I entered to check out there was a man, and his wife just came around a display and I said go ahead of me and they said are you sure and I said yes you only have a few items. As I was still in my uniform and I laid my items on the conveyer the checkout girl started to check my items with the couple in front of me and I said that is my items and she said yes, I know, this man said he wants to pay for your groceries. I said Sr. I will pay for it and his wife came over to me and said my husband said he is going to pay for it. I said ok mam. Now let's look at something. The average Christian would not have delt with this man who had tattoos all over his head and face and dressed in coveralls. Yes, he is a country man. I had $ 24.00 worth of groceries and had the money to pay for it. I thank the man and said God Bless you. Did Jesus Blesse me for praying for our Personnel Manager Cathy just an hour ago. I will let you decide that. The next morning as I was drinking coffee in our breakroom getting ready to go to my post. Here came Cathy headed to the bathroom and she was walking fast, like faster than I ever saw her walk before. She is not a small Sister in Christ. When she came out of the bathroom and grabbed a buggy to take back on the floor, I said Cathy you know who healed you. And she stopped and looked at me and I pointed up toward heaven with my right index finger and said, the "Big Boss" in heaven. She shouted he is "Awesome" Ken and walked out fast and so fast the two employees siting in the breakroom said Ken as long as we have known Cathy, we have never seen her move so quick. I told them as I was headed to the floor, Jesus Healed her. As we look at the healing. First thing was "Compassion" came on me and then "Boldness" and then asking the Lord to forgive us of our sins and then quoting his Holy Scriptures and then telling Jesus let this be a Testimony for your Kingdom. Jesus never has me pray in "Tongues" when praying for someone that needs a healing. Let's talk about the gift of tongues, as you know I went forward in a church service to receive this gift. And like I told you when the Preachers laid hands on me, I received it and it poured out of me so strong I had to stop to get my breath it was so powerful. How does Jesus have me use this gift. I do not "flaunt" this gift from the Holy Ghost. Most people do not know how this gift works. Remember Paul received and was "Filled" with the Holy Ghost when Ananias laid hands on him to get filled and healed. The "Anointing" is transferable, the gift of tongues is transferable by laying on of hands and by someone praying over you to receive this gift. Paul said he spoke in tongues more than anyone. Paul explained the gift as he stated in the Holy Scriptures that you can pray in tongues, speak in tongues, and sing in tongues. Every time during "Praise and Worship" I would pray in tongues and sometimes sing in tongues. This is what it does for me. It raises up my Spirit in me and takes me into the "Supernatural Realm" and then the weightiness, numbness, and Jesus' presence comes on me and I bask in his presence during Praise and Worship. Now at work as a Security / Host at Walmart Supercenter in Cleveland Tn. on Keith St. I would start praying in tongues in a quiet tone and it would build up my spirit and raise it up to a higher level so when the Lord would lead me to a "Divine Appointment" he could use me to pray for someone that needed healing or to cast out a demon or demons. One morning at work I got caught up in the Supernatural Realm praying in tongues and a man came by my post at a fast walk and I saw him and all of a sudden, he stopped in a hurry and turned around and stared at me. He did not say anything to me but just stared at me. I knew he heard something he never heard before. He continued on his way in a hurry to buy something. I'm sure he heard some Hebrew Language, and it got his attention really quick. Jesus is more powerful than most people think. The deep hidden mysteries in the Hebrew Writings tell us that the High Priest at the Temple in Jerusalem on the day of Atonement had to cleanse himself of any sin and could not be with his wife for several days before this Feast. When he walked into the Holy of Holies where the Mercy Seat is, when God showed up between the two Cherub Angels on top of the Mercy Seat, God would start to talk to the High Priest in tongues and the High Priest talked back in tongues to God. When God left the Holy of Holies the High Priest never had the gift of tongues until the following year when he walked back into the Holy of Holies on the day of Atonement.

> 1 Corinthians 12:1
>
> Now concerning spiritual gifts, brethren, I would not have you ignorant.
>
> 1 Corinthians 14: 2 (KJV)
>
> 2 For he that speaketh in an unknown tongue speaketh not unto men, but unto God: for no man understandeth Him; howbeit in the spirit he speaketh mysteries.
>
> 1 Corinthians 14: 4 (KJV)
>
> 4 He that speaketh in an unknown tongue edifieth himself; but he that prophesieth edifieth the church.
>
> I Corinthians 14:14 (KJV)
>
> For if I pray in an unknown tongue, my spirit prayeth, but my understanding is unfruitful.

MORE MIRCALES IN SUPER WALMART CLEVELAND TN. 2017

The first Miracle in Walmart with my boss Keith, we have pictures of me and him where Jesus performed the Miracle. Also, I have pictures of these people that received a Miracle in the store also as I will tell you about how Jesus healed them. The second Miracle with Cathy the Personnel Manager I was not led by the Lord to take a picture of her. One day at the store a man came in struggling to breath at my post by the Pharmacy set of doors. As he walked by slow and stopped every three steps dragging a tank of oxygen with hoses in his nose. When he was about 15 feet from me, I walked over to him, as compassion had come on me as I watched him struggle. I said Sir what are You dealing with and he looked at me and said a lung disease, COPD and I said I'm going to pray for you, and he said I go to "Church" every Sunday and I said that is good. I told him not to say anything when I pray for him, just get in agreement with me. As the Lord led me, I started with Jesus forgive us of our sins, then I started talking to Jesus and I reminded him what he said in the Holy Scriptures about whatever we "Bind and Loose" on earth shall be bound and loosed in heaven. This is one of "Jesus Mysteries" so I said we Bind and Loose that lung diseases away from this man and we "Rebuke" that lung disease away from his lungs in Jesus Name. I said Lord let this be a "Testimony" for you Kingdom Lord, it is all about you Jesus amen. A couple days later the man came back in the store at the Pharmacy doors as I watched him come in and he was walking fast dragging the oxygen tank and hoses. As I looked at him, I said Lord he is getting healed as he was walking without stopping. On his way out of the store he came by as this was a Sunday evening before dark and it stirred my spirit up in me. As he went out the doors, I was led by the Holy Ghost to go talk to him. I ran out to catch him before he left. I said Bro. the

Lord is healing you and he just smiled with the hoses in his nose. I said the next time I see you; the tank and hoses will be gone as you will not need them any more as Jesus is healing you. The next day on Monday morning he walked in without any tank and hoses and he looked great and had a smile on his face. He told me one day he would like to have a picture of me and him. This Miracle changed this man's continence and his way of life and put him closer to the Lord. Thank You Jesus for your Power. When Jesus Disciples said show us how to pray, Jesus said thy Kingdom come thy will be done on earth like it is in heaven. Is there sickness and disease in heaven? He was referring we need to bring his Kingdom Powers from heaven down to the earth.

> Luke 11:1-2 (KJV)
>
> 1 And it came to pass, that, as he was praying in a certain place, when he ceased, one of his disciples said unto him, Lord, teach us to pray, as John also taught his disciples.
>
> 2 And he said unto them, When ye pray, say, Our Father which art in heaven, Hallowed be thy name. Thy kingdom come. Thy will be done, as in heaven, so in earth.

One Sunday as I was at my post checking receipts and Hosting people a man came by me and I said how are you doing today, and he stopped and said I have chest pains and am on heart meds. I said I will pray for you, just get in agreement with me. The Lord always has me ask for forgiveness with the person I'm praying for. I said Jesus you said what we Bind and Loose on earth shall be Bound and Loosed in heaven. I took authority on that holy scripture and we Bind and Loose the chest pains away from this man and Lord restore his heart and let it be a "Testimony" for your Kingdom. It is all about you Jesus. The man said the heart pain quit and the next time I saw him come into the store he said the chest pains have not returned. Thank You Jesus. I took a picture of him. When I would go to work as I was walking across the long parking lot I would talk to Jesus and I burst out laughing, I said Jesus you make me laugh the way you heal these people. That is what is called "Heavenly Laughter" thank you Jesus. In the morning while it was quiet at 7:00 am at my post, I would start praying in "Tongues" and sometimes I would get involved in it and continue to pray and check the customers receipts, they did not know I was praying as I never flaunted the Holy Gift of Tongues. It will build up your spirit in you and raise it to a level that there is "NO UNBELIEF" in you. This is the way Yeshua has led me to pray. My prayer warrior Cathy, she trained me to dispatch the Lord's Angels to help people.

Mark 1:13 (KJV)

13 And he was there in the wilderness forty days, tempted of Satan; and was with the wild beasts; and the angels ministered unto him.

PRAISE AND WORSHIP BREAKS OUT IN SUPER WALMART CLEVELAND TN. ON KEITH ST. 2017

One Sunday afternoon as I was at the grocery doors checking receipts and praying in the spirit something happened as the atmosphere changed while I was praying in the spirit. I heard Praise and Worship Songs and I said Lord is that coming from heaven. I thought it might be Angels singing. Then I heard it behind me in the first set of doors leaving the store. When I looked it was a Gospel Quartet singing songs in the store. They were singing on the way out and stopped between the two set of doors. I could not stand it. I turned around and ran to them and said the Lord did something to me during Praise and Worship, I had a Supernatural Encounter with the Lord in 1998. Don't ever forget Bro's and Sisters I told them, God comes out of the heavens during Praise and Worship. We had church in Walmart. Let's look at something here. Jesus said we are the "LIGHT" on the earth when we become a believer in Jesus Christ. It makes the "DARKNESS" leave. When we "Pray" it changes the atmosphere around us. When we use any one of the "9 Gifts" it raises the Power of Jesus presence to a higher level and causes the darkness to leave. That is bringing God's Kingdom down on earth. Remember what happened at Solomons Temple on the Dedication Day. As the Levite Priest blew 120 Shofars and the cymbals and instruments of music and they lifted up their voice, God showed up in a cloud in the Temple and the Priest hit the floor because they fell under the Power of God's presence.

2 Chronicles 5: 12-14 (KJV)

12 Also the Levites which were the singers, all of

them of Asaph, of Heman, of Jeduthun, with their

sons and their brethren, being arrayed in white linen, having

cymbals and psalteries and harps, stood at the east end of the

altar, and with them an hundred and twenty priests sounding

with trumpets:

14 So that the priests could not stand to minister by

reason of the cloud: for the glory of the Lord had filled the
house of God

Psalm 150: 1-6 (KJV)

1 Praise ye the Lord. Praise God in his sanctuary: praise him

In the firmament of his power.

2 Praise him for his mighty acts: praise him according to his

excellent greatness.

3 Praise him with the sound of the trumpet: praise him with

The psaltery and harp.

4 Praise him with the timbrel and dance: praise him with
stringed

Instruments and organs.

5 Praise him upon the loud cymbals: praise him upon the high

sounding cymbals.

6 Let every thing that hath breath praise the Lord. Praise ye
the Lord.

JESUS TAKES CARE OF HIS SERVANTS 2017
THE NEW DENTIST SAID I HAVE NEVER SEEN THIS BEFORE

Cathy woke me up at 7:00 am and said Ken call Dr. Beard's office as I was tired, and I called the Dentist Office like they told me to. It wrang busy so I went back to sleep and Cathy said Ken call them again. So, I did, and the receptionist answered, and I told her who I was, and she said ken can you come in today at 3:30 pm and I said I'm sorry I do not get off work until 4:00 pm and she said Ken we close at 4:00 pm we will try and take you next time. The "LIGHT ON THE EARTH" is Jesus Kingdom on earth, he functions in the "SUPERNATURAL REALM". After I hung the phone up the receptionist called me back and said can you get here at 3:50 pm and I said yes. She said we will be waiting on you. I asked my Boss at Walmart is there any way I can get off early for a dentist appointment I need to be there at 3:50 pm and he said sure I will let you off 30 minutes so you can get there in time. When I walked in for my appointment, they X-rayed my teeth and wow what new Technology they have, it is State of the Art. The dental hygienist said open your mouth and as she held a small flat plate with a cord attached to it to the big screen, she pushed a button and bam all my teeth was on the big screen in front of me. Dr. Ken Beard the Son said you have "NO CAVITIES" and I have never seen this before? You have 3 broken teeth and there is "NO CAVITIES" trying to form on those broken teeth. I did not say anything as the former Dentist told me the same thing last year. Dr. Ken Beard takes his hands and places them under his arm pits and said what do you want me to do for you. I said Doc whatever you want to do. He looked at his Staff and said let's fix these broken teeth. We will do a root canal on two of the broken teeth and put a special compound on the one broken tooth. I said Doc no pain and he said there is no pain in this Dentistry. Three of them went to work on me and there was "NO PAIN". Wow Jesus is Powerful. When they finished up Dr. Ken Beard looked at his Team and said we just set a record we did all of this in 45 minutes. And then they cleaned my teeth for me. God doesn't charge his Servants when he wants to take care of them. God new I did not have the finances to pay for this. During the Healing Outpouring in Lakeland, Florida I witnessed some people felt something in their mount and they received a Gold Filling Supernaturally as I watched and Millions around the World. Me and Cathy do not put God in a Box. Thank You Jesus. "What happened to the "Churches" and "Preachers" today? Look around do you see "Dead" Churches, no Signs, Wonders, Miracles, Salvation, taking place. The Lord has showed since I Repented of my Sins and accepted Jesus Christ as my Lord and Savior how satan works through people just like In the Bible. When he comes into a Church and shows up. It is called a "Religious Controlling Spirit" when he is there. It stops the movement of the "Holy Ghost" and his Power. This Spirit of Evil can come on a Priest or a Preacher and they are not aware of it. Remember when Jesus and Peter were walking along as Peter said nothing is going to happen to you. And the response was" But he turned, and said unto Peter, Get thee behind me, Satan: thou art an offence unto me: (Matt. 16:23).

JESUS CONTINUES TO DO MIRACLES IN SUPER WALMART KEITH ST CLEVELAND TN. 2018

One day at the Garden Center Post one of our employees walked by and I said how are you doing today, and she said I have severe pain in my eyes. As she continued to work, she came back by and I said do you still have the pain and she said yes, I may have to go home. I said let me pray for you and she said yes. I told her just get in agreement with me as I talk to the Lord. As I started talking, I said Lord forgive us our sins, and Lord this lady needs your help, her eyes have a pain in them, and she needs to work. Lord send your Angels and take care of her and we Rebuke that pain in her eyes away from her in Jesus Name. She went back to work in the Garden Center and when she came back by, she said the pain left her eyes. That is a Miracle and I told her to thank Jesus for healing her. Another day at the Grocery Door Post a man came up to me in a wheelchair and said remember when you prayed for me and I said Bro. inform me and he said I had heart failure and after you prayed for me the Doctors said my heart was 30 % stronger since you prayed. I said thank Jesus for healing you. Today April 10, 2021 I had to by something at Walmart and one of my pears Elijah a Security / Host said Ken remember the man you prayed for that had two walkers. He still comes in the store without the walkers. I said thank you Jesus. The Baptism of the Holy Ghost is very Powerful, Jesus Commanded them to receive that Power.

The Holy Ghost spoke to me three times in Super Walmart at my Security Post. Write a book about my Kingdom. This is the book the Lord wanted me to write. All through the bible the Lord speaks to his people in an Audible Voice, and in Visions and Dreams. Jesus Christ is the same yesterday, today and forever.

HEADED TO OUR GRANDSON'S GRADUATION A SECRET GOVERNMENT COMPOUND OCT. 30 - 2018

Only 6 family members could attend the Graduation. The only ones allowed on the grounds are the President and his Staff. The morning we arrived was clear and the Sun was rising. I was taking photos with my I phone, and Zachary's wife's grandfather George said Ken

you look like a Professional Photographer. Yes, I was excited as me and Cathy and all the families and friends were praying for Zachary on his journey as three Government men about 4 months prior walked up to him months after he received his bachelor's degree in "Criminology" at South Eastern University in Lakeland, Florida. And the Government men said we have chosen you, as we only picked 24 out of "150,000" people. Remember in an earlier chapter how a Professor from a Christian University, Lee University, Tn. felt the Anointing on a young man walking by his vehicle to go into McDonalds in Ga. and the Professor handed him his book he wrote, how to guard the Anointing. During the Graduation Ceremony I could not help but to weep as we watched Zachary received his Award from our Government Commanders and after words, I walked outside and the Big Black Armored Lumazine called the "TANK" was there and I walked up to it and took pictures of it. The area is so wild, the deer walked up about 20 yards away from us. We bought items that no one can buy unless you have a family member Graduate from this Agency. We walked along where the former Presidents walked on this site. I will never forget watching Zachary achieve what the Lord called him to do. It was very "Exciting" to say the least. They took pictures of me and Zachary at this Graduation and we can't post them on any Media for protection. The next day we went to see the White House for the first time walking down Pennsylvania Ave. early in the morning. When God wants something done, he picks who he wants to achieve it for him to protect and reach Souls for his Kingdom even in High Places.

GOD OPENS UP MORE DOORS 9 - 2018

When you become a Believer in Jesus Christ get ready for his movement and favor for you when you are not expecting it to happen. The day after Zachary's Graduation as we were walking down Pennsylvania Ave. and when we walked by the Eisenhower Building our granddaughter Casey yelled here comes Zachary and we looked and here he was walking across Pennsylvania Ave. to go on his assignment. We gave him a hug and who can make those arrangements but our Heavenly Father. The White House area is very clean and the huge stone buildings are astonishing and beautiful. Casey asked her friend don't you have a family member that works at the Capital Building and she said yes. Casey said see if you can get my Grandfather and Mom and Dad access to it. Wow God opens another door for us. The next day we had Access to the Capital Building with a "Personal Tour" inside. I never thought I would ever see the White House and Capital and Supreme Court and walk up to them. God is up to something?

GOD CONTINUES TO SHOW ME EVIL / CORRUPTION

As we were guided on a personal tour in the Capitol Building in DC it was an honor to walk up the steps and onto the first floor where our first President George Washington and Abraham Lincoln walked in. We were told the first floor is the original floor and we took pictures as we walked with the big pillars there on the first floor. As we headed down one of the hallways, we came to Florida State Flag outside the office, and we were escorted into the Congressman's office and as we sat down at a long table to our left and in front of us was the Congressman's Assistance a young man. I had my back to him, and our Son asked him a question is the Congressman in and he said no he is in Florida. Our Son said yes, it is Election Day today in Florida. Our Son said I'm sure he is coming against Nelson today. And the young intern said no he will not say anything bad about him, they are "CLOSE FRIENDS". How can you hold a position for the people and claim to be a Christian and not come against someone who supports Killing Babies and is a Liberal? Now I know why this Republican Congressman did not become our President of US and I know Religious Leaders call this Florida Congressman a Christian. How can you be a Christian and not challenge the adversary who sits in the Congress and State Capitol and not say anything. Wow this was an eye opener to me. As we continued the tour with the College Student guiding us, we came to a room with "Huge Paintings" on the wall. I asked the guide are these pictures the original and she said yes. The young college girl showed us a picture where the presentation of the draft of the Declaration of Independence to Congress. One of the Congressman had his foot on another Congressman's foot as he was talking. The Canvas Oil paintings looked so real. Then we looked around at all the pictures and Bust of George Washington. Then we went to the

Capitol Rotunda and we took pictures. Our Son said Dad look at all the "Deities" on the top of the Dome and I said to myself, now I know why we have good Godly Presidents and Evil Presidents. When you have Demons painted and sculptured you are asking for trouble. This is sad to say the least. Now I know why there was only one President of the United States to allow "JESUS CHRIST NAME" at the White House and it was our President I voted for, President Donald Trump who God placed over "SIX PROPHECIES" on starting in 2011 – 2016. When God's people cried out, Lord who do we vote for as they were in a Pagan Nation in the book of Isaiah 45. When God heard their cries, he spoke back and said I placed my hand of "CYRUS" and God's people "MURMURED" and when God heard them, he said I have "ANOINTED CYRUS" and he does not know me, but he will. Cyrus was not a believer he did not know who God was. He also was a "Builder" and not a "Politician" like Donald Trump. Cyrus became a Believer in God and he removed the "Gates of Hell" from God's people and told them they could leave and go home to Israel and rebuild the Temple for God. Do you see the parallel today and what happened in 2020? It is a shame how Religious Leaders came against our President Donald Trump. God Exposed them on Media and it makes me sick. I will go into more detail about what God has showed me later. The White House area is very clean and kept up very well. It is an honor to do the Lord's work in this place as our grandson made sure I rode with him to work and he would drop me off at 5 :30 am, I will never forget it and the people I met walking down Pennsylvania Ave in front of the White House and Eisenhower Building and the Greatest President we ever had. It hurst me to know what has happened as I'm writing this today on April 20, 2021.

THE VOICE SAID BLOW THE SHOFAR AT THE WHITE HOUSE

On Jan 4, 2019, I opened my Bible to study over a cup of Coffee, it opened to Judges chapter 6. Then I heard the voice of the Holy Ghost say to me, go to the White House and Blow the "Shofar". I heard this voice three times. I told Zachary that day what happened to me when he arrived home. He said Pawpaw I can drop you off when I go to work just let me know then I can pick you up after work. So, we went on Jan. 8, 2019, and I walked up 17th St. and crossed Pennsylvania Ave. to get some coffee at McDonalds to study the Bible. I laid my Shofar and Bible on the table and Black Brim hat. Then I headed out walked across the street and walked in front of the White House and first I prayed, repenting for those who come against God's Laws and our President Donald Trump. Then I sounded the Shofar 3 times and then walked down Pennsylvania Ave. to 15th St. by the Treasury Dept. and then to the back side of the White House and stood and prayed and repented for those who come against God's Laws and our President Donald Trump and sounded the Shofar 3 times and then headed toward the Capital Building as the Sun Rise was coming over the Supreme Court Building. and I looked down at my bible and started reading it tells how Gideon was worried and God sent one of his Angels to tell him fear not, thou shalt not die. Then God speaks to Gideon and said throw down the Altar of "Ba'al" that your father hath. Then the Spirit of the Lord came upon Gideon, and he blew the "Shofar". Then Gideon and his men "Blew the Shofar's" and the enemy ran, cried, and started killing each other with God's weapon. As the Shofar sounded on Jan. 8, 2019 all over the White House area and the sound echoed off the buildings and what happened when God's weapon changed the Atmosphere. The next day on Fox News Jim Acosta from CNN was at the Southern Border New Wall and said

President Donald Trump said there was thousands of people at the Border. He said there is no one here at the New Wall. A Jewish Attorney for our President Donald Trump Jay Sekulow stated on Fox News that what Jim Acosta said about no people at the New Wall, sealed our President to continue to build the wall. Jim Acosta was bragging on the wall. All the major Press is in the White House before they head out and they had to have heard the "Sound of the Shofar" echoing off the building. What happened over 2,000 years ago in the Bible when the Shofars sounded around the enemy camp of over 30,000 of the enemy? They screamed and ran and started crying and killing each other. Remember what the Holy Scripture said. Jesus Christ is the same yesterday, today, and forever. He has not changed. Then on Feb. 9, 2019 I was led by the Holy Ghost to go back and continue to do the Lord's work and I go with Zachary and he dropped me off around 5:15 am and I had Jesus weapons with me again the Holy Bible and Shofar and Anointing Oil from Israel. This time the Holy Ghost led me to sound the "Shofar" at all the same locations and now in front of the "Department of Justice and FBI Buildings" as I headed to the Capital and Supreme Court and pray and repent for those coming against our President and God's Laws and asking the Lord to release his Angels in these buildings and clean up the corruption. At about 10:00 am when Zachary took his break, we had coffee and a breakfast snack something I will never forget. Here I am a country boy from Dade City, Florida doing the Lord's work in DC meeting Attorneys and High Officials as I walked by the White House and Eisenhower Buildings and they would say to me we like your hat as I wore a black flat brim hat and carried the Shofar and the bible and sounded it when the Holy Ghost led me. The street people would say to me we like your hat also. The Muslims would look at me and then turned their head and would say nothing. That's ok they knew I was a Servant of the Lord.

THE SOUND OF GOD'S WEAPON CHANGES THE ATMOSPHERE FEB. 9, 2019

Each mission the Lord had me on in DC was amazing to say the least. On this second trip to the White House on Feb. 9, 2019 as Zachary dropped me off around 5:30 am on 17th St. and I would walk by the Eisenhower Building and cross Pennsylvania Ave. to go to McDonalds for Breakfast and Coffee, and I would study the Holy Scriptures before I would head out to do the Lord's work. I then walk across to the White House and stand in front of it on Pennsylvanian Ave. and Pray and Repent for those coming against our President Donald Trump who God Anointed like Cyrus in the Bible. Then I would ask the Lord to release his Angels around the White House for protection for President Trump and his family and all his Staff as it has been a battle for him to clean up America. I would release the sound of the Shofar with three blast and then another set of blast from the Shofar. Then I would head down Pennsylvania Ave to the Treasury Building on 15th St. and then head South and I would walk to the South end of the White House and set up and Pray and Repent and asked the Lord to release his Angels to the White House to protect our President and his wife and Staff. Then I would go back to 15th St. and head to the Capital as you could see it 16 blocks away. On the way I would stop and pray at the FBI Building and sound the Shofar asking the Lord to send his Angels inside it and clean up the corruption. The Shofar would echo off the building all over the street alongside of it. Then I would continue to walk to the Capital, and I would stop at the Department of Justice Building and stand 20 feet from it and prayed and repented for those coming against the truth. Then I would head to the Capital Building and watch the "Big Black SUV's" drive up and I would pray and repent and release the Alarm of the Shofar. And release the sound again and again and then I would go across the street to the Supreme Court Building and pray and repent for those coming against God's Laws and ask the Lord to send his Angels and bring Justice to America. When I was through, I would catch a cab and head back to the White House area and eat lunch and rest over a cup of coffee at the cafe and then head to the Park on Pennsylvania Ave. and relax and meditate. When me and Zachary arrived at his place and Cathy asked me how it went, and I told her. At times I would have her pray while doing the Lord's work. On a news clip that evening it stated "Melania Trump" said I'm not going back into that White Building until those "Demon Idols" are removed that the Clintons and Obama put there. The Shofar is a weapon of God's.

HOW POWERFUL IS THE NAME OF JESUS?

One morning as I was headed to the Capital Building, I used a Cab leaving the back side of the Treasury Department and the Holy Ghost started to work through me. I asked the Cab driver if he was from here and he said no that he was from "Ethiopia" and I said I met a Bishop who is over the Church of God of Prophecy in Ethiopia. I met him in Walmart in Cleveland Tn as a Security / Host at Walmart. I asked him what is going on in your "Neck of the Woods" Bishop and he said his Country was under persecution for 28 years and God placed a New Prime Minister who loves Jesus. Wow that is good news, he went on to say he is helping the people like President Trump. The Cab driver got excited and asked me do you like Jesus and I said I'm a Servant of his and he shouted amen and said he was a Jesus man. The Holy Ghost is Powerful when you turn him loose to help you. The Cab driver went into detail about their New Prime Minister Abiy Ahmed. He said he was a Muslim and at a Socker Game in Middle School when Abiy was 15 years old someone walked up to him after the game and said, "JESUS IS LORD, JESUS IS LORD, JESUS IS LORD" and when Abiy went home all he could think about was Jesus is Lord and when he went to sleep all he heard was Jesus is Lord. The next day he accepted Jesus Christ as his Savior. On April 2, 2018 Abiy Ahmed was elected Prime Minister of Ethiopia and has turned their Country around. Thank You Jesus. The Holy Ghost is Powerful and show you things behind the scenes. The Cab driver wanted to hear the Shofar so when I arrived at the Capital and Supreme Court, I sounded the Shofar, and he was Praising Jesus and drove off. God has put a lot of people in my path doing his work for his Kingdom on Earth.

HOW TO COME AGAINST AN EVIL FORCE WHILE STUDYING THE LORD'S WORD

One morning before I headed out to do the Lord's work, I stopped by to get some coffee while studying the Holy Scriptures in McDonalds across from the White House and Eisenhower Buildings with my shofar laying in front of me on the table, and the Holy Bible and a Muslim man came in and was very rude with people, asking them for money and he was talking in his Arabic language at times. I saw what he was doing, and he saw the Shofar and Bible on my table and me studying. He came over to me and as soon as he did, I started praying in "Tongues" and as soon as he heard God's language he turned away and never came back over to me again and then left McDonalds. The Holy Gifts is Powerful. There are Nine Gifts from the Lord. Paul said to the Christians, now concerning spiritual gifts, brethren, I would not have you "IGNORANT". The gifts Paul was talking about in the Holy Scriptures are diversities of gifts, but the same Spirit. Here they are. The gift of Wisdom, Word of Knowledge, Faith, Healing, Miracles, Prophecy, Discerning of spirits, Diverse Tongues, Interpretation of Tongues. It is all the same Spirit and God which worketh all in all. The Evil forces hate the Light of Jesus Christ. Why do you think Jesus Christ told his people not to leave Jerusalem until they receive the "Baptism of the Holy Ghost" and Jesus said John Baptized with Water and I will Baptize you with the Holy Ghost not many days from now to give you more Power? At the Park on Pennsylvania Ave in front of the White House is I was sitting on the Park bench resting from doing the Lord's work and a crowd formed and a lady was waving our American Flag facing the Park across the street and in front of her were Protestors with their Flags from Turkey as it had the Crescent Moon on it, and they were light blue, and I called Cathy and said the Crescent Moon on these Flags represents the Muslims even thow they are blue she said yes. They were chanting against our President and mocking him and waving their Flags toward our American Flag. The Holy Ghost led me to blow the Shofar 3 times and the Muslims took down their Flags and left. Thank You Jesus for your Power in the Shofar. The Rabbis came wearing "Red Trump" hats walking down Pennsylvania Ave as I asked to get a picture and they said sure. One morning headed to do the Lord's work at the White House, Zachary dropped me off at the "Trump International Tower" and I went into the Coffee Shop and laid my weapons down the Shofar and Bible and studied while drinking a fresh cup of coffee. Then I headed out praying and blowing the Shofar at the FBI Building and Department of Justice asking the Lord to send his Angels to clean up the corruption. A group of Attorneys walking in the side of the Department of Justice all turned and looked when they heard God's Weapon sound.

> Numbers 10:9 (KJV)
>
> And if you go to war in your land against
>
> the enemy that oppresseth you, then you
>
> shall blow an alarm with the trumpets; and
>
> ye shall be remembered before the Lord your
>
> God, and ye shall be saved from your enemies.

WHITE HOUSE JAN. 28, 2020 SOUNDING THE SHOFAR BENJAMIN NETANYAHU IS HERE SIGNING THE DEAL OF A LIFETIME

As I was continuing to do the Lord's work in DC, starting at the White House sounding the Shofar on the North end and South end and at the Department of Justice and FBI building and at the Capital Building and Supreme Court, as I rested up for lunch I saw a group of Rabbi's and their family standing on the corner of Pennsylvania Ave. and 17 th Street, I was led by the Holy Ghost to walk over and talk to the Chief Rabbi about the 3 rd. Temple being built. As I was standing there waiting guess who came walking by and I yelled Preacher and he stopped and looked at me and walked over to me as I had the Shofar and Black brim hat on, it was Pastor Robert Jeffress, and he gave me a "Fist Bump" with a smile as he was in a hurry to go to the White House as the Prime Minister Benjamin Netanyahu was here to Sign the Deal of a Lifetime. The "Israel – Arab" peace accord was signed, thank you Jesus for our President Donald Trump. As me and the Chief Rabbi talked about the original Temple Site was found in the City of David about 1'000 feet south of what is called the Temple Mount and it is just like the Holy Scriptures state it was where the only source of "WATER" was in Jerusalem, the Gihon Spring.

GOD EXPOSED THE CHURCH SECRET APRIL 5, 2020

As the World saw the Capital of Israel Sealed and Jesus Name allowed at the White House since 2016 with our President Donald Trump for the first time and bringing peace with the signing of the Israel – Arab peace accord and Jesus is getting closer to his return I found out a "SECRET" the Evangelist and Preachers kept to themselves. On April 5, 2020 I received the book called "THE TRUMP PROPHECIES" by Bro. Mark Taylor. I was listening to him since 2018 while doing the Lord's work at the White House. Now he goes into detail about how God spoke to him in a "Audible Voice" in 2011 and Donald Trump will become President of US. Bro. Mark Taylor is a retired Lieutenant from the Fire Department. He had a Supernatural Encounter with the Lord and "Electricity" ran through his body. Remember the experience I had in 1998 that changed me forever. Well, this caught my eye about Bro. Mark Taylor, he is a friend of mine. I never could understand as a Catholic and a Sophomore in High School why the Priests did not speak about the Federal Law "PRAYER IN SCHOOLS" in America is not allowed anymore. Not a word about it in the Sanctuary in 1960. Then the Federal Law was passed and now "KILLING BABIES / ABORTION" in America is allowed. WHAT, WHAT, I accepted Jesus Christ as my Savior in Jan. 1969 and the Preachers were quiet in the Sanctuary about it. WHY, WHY, then in 2015 the Federal Law passed "SAME SEX MARRIAGE", WHAT, WHAT, and then in 2016 an Evangelist we were associated with said I'm going to invite Donald Trump, Ted Cruz, Marco Rubio, who were running for the President of the United States and have them come and speak to us. We were excited because the Holy Ghost showed me that God had placed over "SIX PROPHECIES" on Donald Trump and he will be President of United States. Then the Evangelist on the second week said well I can invite anyone

I want here. I even rent this building out. I knew in my Spirit someone was complaining. Then the third week he stood before us and said the Federal Government contacted me and said if one word is out of order, we will pull down this Ministry. I sat there and said to myself how can one word shut this Ministry down? Then it hit the Air Ways and in this book. God Warned his Churches to come out of that "FEDERAL CONTRACT" the Evangelist and Preachers signed up for. Let me explain it to you. In 1954 a Senator by the name of Lyndon B. Johnson proposed the amendment called the "501c3 Johnson Amendment". The churches were already getting "FREE TAXES" on their church buildings and land. This New Amendment gave them more "FREE MONEY" with no taxes on all the money coming into the churches if they signed up for it. My expression, they ran to it like a "Herd of Cattle" for more Free Money. Everything went well as the money was flowing and something happened in 1960 and 1973 and 2015. It's called the "FEDERAL LAW CONTRACT" if you come against the Federal Laws in the Sanctuary and the Government finds out about it, they will pull your "FREE MONEY CONTRACT" the 501c3 that is connected to the "BAAL SPIRIT" controlled by Abortion in DC. This "501c3 UMBRELLA" has the "CHURCH OF SATAN" and the rest of the Cult Religions under it also. How can a Pastor or Evangelist Serve Jesus Christ while holding hands with satan? God placed the Warning out in 2017 about coming out from the 501c3 and then something happened. A Plague shut all the Church Doors all over the World as God watches the Plague and as God watches some of his "Religious Leaders" come against our President Donald Trump and look at the weak support from most Preachers for our President Donald Trump who God appointed to clean up America and the corruption as Jesus is getting closer to his return for the catching away or Rapture and his return to Jerusalem Israel. An estimated 22,000 Christians did not Vote in 2020. God has been "Exposing" Corrupt Leaders in DC and the Pedophile Ring Leaders in DC and even in his Churches as the World watches. I will continue to Serve the Lord and watch what God is going to do next as I know he is not happy when some of these same Religious Leaders that turned against him ran to the Federal Government Fund the PPP and some reached in and pulled out "4.7 Million – 1.7 Million" as our President was getting ready to Leave Office. It looks like they got "BARABBAS" and they do not know what to do with him? All my life from age 14 years old to 72 years old I could never figure out what they were hiding. "NOW WE KNOW THE SECRET". God said he will pull down his corrupt Religious Leaders in Mark Taylors book and Expose them. After the Lord had me do in DC and watch how God Exposed the Corrupt Religious Leaders, that raised their voice against our President Trump on his New Immigration Bill, the Religious Leader from Ga. said he needs needs "Compassion" on the Immigrants? Then when President stated in a Tweet, Riots cause killings, this Preacher stood raised his voice, our President needs to have "Compassion" for the people Rioting. Other Religious Leaders from Tx marched with Black Lives, Matter. Three more Religious Leaders a Lady her books are in the Christian Book Stores stood and said I'm pro life don't vote for Trump two Pastors said the same thing. God sees everything and they cant hide from Him? They got "Barabbas" and do not know what to do with him. They Rejected God's Warning to remove themselves from the "501c3" the "BAAL" spirit and Abortion controls it in DC. They signed a contract for it.

MORE MIRACLES TAKE PLACE IN 2020 JESUS IS THE HEALER

Before we left Alexandria Va. I had a Dentistry Shiny Dental Dr. Tina N. Truong at 6377 Little River Trnpk. Alexandria, VA 22312 one "July 17, 2020" to X Ray my teeth and clean them. The X Ray showed "Seven Cavities" and below the teeth under the gums needs cleaning. What happened Lord, I need your help again, what went wrong. We headed back to Cleveland Tn. on July 24, 2020 to our Log Cabin and on "Nov. 6, 2020" at 9:30 am I went to Dr. Brian Beard, Center for Cosmetic Dentistry to get my teeth cleaned and "X Rayed" and they said Ken you have only "One Cavity" and we will repair it for you and clean your teeth. WHAT, WHAT, where did the other "6 Cavities" go and the gum tarter below. They Disappeared by the "SUPERNATURAL POWER" of Jesus Christ, this is the "SUPERNATURAL REALM" where he functions, and it is available on earth to all Believers in Jesus Christ. Why do you think Jesus said to Pray, Thy Kingdom Come, Thy Will Be Done on Earth as it is in Heaven? In Heaven is where Jesus sits on the right hand of the Father. What we just saw is the "LIGHT ON THE EARTH" verses "DARKNESS ON THE EARTH". All through the Bible we see Signs, Wonders, Miracles, Salvation. Nothing has changed but the Church Leaders and Denominations. Why did Jesus say I'm the same yesterday, today, and forever? The Religious Leaders threw out the Power Gifts or they do not believe in them or there is a "RELIGIOUS SPIRIT" in there Church somewhere.

Hebrew 13:8 (KJV)

Jesus Christ the same yesterday, and to day, and for ever.

Luke 11:2 (KJV)

And he said unto them, When ye pray, say, Our Father which art in heaven, Hallowed be thy name. Thy will be done, as in heaven, so in earth.

Mark 4:11 (KJV)

And he said unto them, Unto you it is given to Know the mystery of the kingdom of God: but unto Them that are without, all [these] things are done in Parables:

HOW POWERFUL IS JESUS KINGDOM ON EARTH

1.

Let's look back on what happened to me. At Enterprise Missionary Baptist Church, Pastor Johnie Osborne led me in the Sinners Prayer at the Altar and I Repented of my Sins and accepted Jesus Christ as my Lord and Savior and then I was Baptized by Pastor Johnie Osborne in Pretty Pond in Zephyrhills Florida on September 13, 1969. As a Believer I'm in Jesus "Royal Priesthood". It is a "Honor" to be in "THE KINGDOM PRIESTHOOD".

2.

Then in 1998 in a Southern Baptist Church in Blanton, Florida I received a powerful Revalation that the Thief comes to Steal, Kill, and Destroy you.

3.

Then at this same Southern Baptist Church during Praise and Worship some Boldness came on me and I pointed to Bro. Donny who was raising his hands toward heaven during "Praise and Worship" at the end of the Service after Altar call and I said Lord that man Loves you, so do I and I said Lord I have never tried this before. I'm going to raise my hands towards heaven. When I did the Power of Jesus Christ came upon me and it started on the tips of my fingers like "Electricity" and then it came down through my body. I asked the Lord what this is. Then a "Tingling" sensation came upon me and down through my body and then a "Numbness" came upon my body and then Jesus' "Weightiness" came upon me and came down through my body.

4.

About two weeks later the Brothers at the Church said Stone is coming to town, Brooksville Florida. I told Cathy with a Name like Stone that is Powerful. The Holy Ghost led us to see what this Evangelist had to say. He walked out on the platform and said I'm not a Prophet. But the Lord does reveal things to me at times and then quoted (Amos 3:7). Surely the Lord God will do nothing, but he revealeth his secret unto his servants the prophets. He Preached about the "5 Chambers of Hell" and the "Fallen Angels". I told Cathy, WOW, WOW, are we in Church.

5.

Then a few weeks after that I received the "Baptism of the Holy Ghost" that John the Baptist and Jesus spoke about to give you more "POWER" to do Jesus' work on earth to reach Souls.

6.

The Evangelist Preached about the Power in God's Weapons the "SHOFAR" and "ANOINTING OIL" and the "PRAYER SHAWL".

7.

Jesus showed me how to raise up my "SPIRIT" inside of me, the Holy Ghost to a higher level and at times went into the "Supernatural Realm" where his Power is by praying in "TONGUES" and he always had me talk to him personally and tell him the Holy Scripture he quoted in the Bible. He did not have me Pray in Tongues to heal someone. When Pastor Cutshall heard about the "Miracles" taking place in Cleveland Tn. at Walmart on Keith St. with 381 Churches in Town and Jesus did not have me pray in Tongues over them, he said that is very Interesting.

8.

Jesus showed me he likes me to talk to him. Jesus showed me how to "PRAY" for the Sick by "DIVINE APOINTMENT" by talking to him and "REPENTING" first and then "REMINDING" him what he said in the Holy Scriptures and having that person I'm praying for to be "QUIET" and getting in agreement with "US". Don't forget when there is "THREE OF US" there is Power.

9.

My Beautiful wife Cathy who is behind the scenes and my "PRAYER WARROR" from day one and who always told me, Ken the only way into Heaven you must accept "JESUS CHRIST" she never beat me up for being a Catholic. She has showed me how to "ANOINT" with "ANOINTING OIL" from Israel. And it is "POWERFUL" when you "PLEAD THE BLOOD OF JESUS CHRIST" over the Anointing Oil from Israel. Remember the Testimony of the huge Demon that came out of the Attack in the Doctor's Office.

SOME IMPORTANT PEOPLE GOD PUT IN MY PATH

1. MASTER CARVER MOONEY ERNEST WARTHER

   - He carved me a pair of plyers out of a solid block of wood. He carved Train Locomotives out of Ivory.

2. WORLD RECORD LARGE MOUTH BASS.

   - Fritz Friebel from San Antonio, Florida is the first one to hold the World Record. This true story begins with me dispatched on a trouble ticket to a house in San Antonio Florida in 1974, to repair a ringer on a wall telephone. I was assigned by the Telephone Company, at the time, to maintain the San Antonio 588 exchange and I was 27 years old. The trouble ticket was for Mr. Walter Friebel who lived across the street from the San Antonio Park and the Catholic Middle School. After I fixed the ringer and went to my truck to place my tools back Mr. Walter Friebel followed me out. When I was getting ready to leave as you never know when the Holy Ghost may need you to say something about the Lord. Not far down the street was Clear Lake in the neighborhood and being an avid fisherman all my life and associated with Great Bass Fisherman like Hoppy who was the Best Bass Fly Fisherman in America at the time and who caught Bass up to 12 pounds and he showed me how to Fly Fish for Bass and skull a boat with a six-foot oar and my Dad who caught Bass up to 18 pounds. I asked Mr. Walter Friebel if he did any fishing in this neck of the woods and he said yes until his brother Fritz caught the World Record Large Mouth Bass. He said they only had one rod and reel and one paddle, and his brother Fritz would do the fishing. I asked him would you mind telling me about it. I asked him was it in the morning or evening and what kind of bait did he use. Mr. Friebel said It was on a Sunday morning and we should have been in church. They went to "Big Fish Lake" and about 10:00 am his brother through the fishing bait toward some Lilly Pads and when he did a Huge Fish struck the bait and he said it took him 20 minutes to bring it in. He went on to say they came back to the town of San Antonio to weigh the Giant fish at the Town Market with the Federal Scales. It weighed "20 pounds. 2 ounces" and 31 inches long and with a 27- inch girth. Standing outside some of the Towns people said when they saw the fish that his brother put some lead weights in it. While standing their Fritz took his pocketknife and split the Huge Bass stomach open and said see there is no led weights in this bass. Mr. Friebel went on to tell me that Fritz wrote a letter to Field and Stream, and they recognized the Bass as the first "World Record Large Mouth Bass" as Fritz told them how he weighed the fish at the Town Market in San Antonio on their Federal Scales. He told Field and Stream he caught the fish in Moody Lake and on a "Creek Chub Pike Minnow". The reason he did not tell them he caught it in Big Fish Lake was to keep other people from fishing at Big Fish Lake. He went on to tell me that Field and Stream sent his brother several Lanterns and Fishing Equipment and Cooking Equipment. He also said the Huge Fish was placed in a block of Ice in a Hardware Store in Tampa; Florida called "Nights Hardware Store" for people to come by to see it. All the old timers at the time did not know about the Big Fish. As I spread the good news a Sportswriter from the Tampa Tribune wrote an article about it when he heard about it and placed a "Marker" at the Town Park with Fredrick Joseph "Fritz" Friebel on it and "Florida's Record Bass". On the Marker it states it was caught in May of 1923 and Fedrick Joseph "Fritz" Friebel (1893 – 1965) I'm glad I was used to spread the news and the Sportswriter searched it out and placed a Marker for the Town of San Antonio and letting me meet Mr. Walter Friebel. Thank You Jesus.

3. SMOKEY YUNICK

- The Great Race Car and Engine Builder and he had a "Photographic Memory". It started out a friend of mine Ronald Northrip in Boot Camp said Ken, I know Smokey Yunick and I can get you and your brothers on the infield for the 1967 Daytona Nascar Race. Smokey has his 1967 Chevelle with the "427 Mystery" engine in it. This was my first Nascar Race attendance, and I was 21 years old and Buzzie Reutimann 00 mentioned Smokey Yunick to me before this race. We headed to the Daytona Speedway and Ronald took us by Smokey's place and we stopped as this section was fenced off. As we looked, we saw a Black Chevelle with the hood up and we could see the orange motor with three two-barrel carbs on it and we thought it was the car for the Big Race. It wasn't, it was a spare race car. When we arrived at the racetrack and walked out into the infield there sitting on the Pole position was the Black and Gold # 13 race car of Smokey's. It was the only car on the track at that moment and I walked out to the track and stood about 10 feet from the car and just staired at it. I could have walked down to meet Smokey and did not think about it. The race started and I will never forget how the # 13 Chevelle led the pack for 20 laps, and I told my brother and the rest of the guys with us, I can close my eyes and point out the "Mystery Engine" and I covered my eyes and pointed at it as it went around the track. That Big Block 427 was "Screaming High RPM" as it led the race for 20 laps as Curtis Turner poured the coal to her. Richard Petty's (426 Hemi) could only get 6 car lengths behind the Mystery Engine. Smokey's car went in for a pit stop and he adjusted something under the hood and Curtis floor boarded the big engine as he was a lap behind because of the pit stop. He caught up and then when he came out of number 4 turn blue smoke came out from Black and Gold # 13. A connecting rod broke as Smokey told GM the rods need to be heavier, and they would not listen.

THE PHONE CALL TO SMOKEY YUNICK 1967
427 Z-11 engine Verses 427 Mystery engine

Months after the Daytona Race, GM shipped Buzzie Reutimann a 425 hp 396 engine and he sold the Big 430 cui 409 engine to my brother who worked in the Parts Department at the Chevy Gurage for them. This would have been the first Big Block Chevy engine Buzzie was going to race, instead the Factory sent him the 396 engine for the 1/3 mile oval race track in Tampa, Florida. So, I called Smokey Yunick and he answered the call and I said, Mr. Yunick do you have a 427 Z-11 crankshaft and he said yes, I have three of them. The next question I asked him what can you tell me about the Chevy 427 Z-11 engine and the Chevy 427 Mystery engine and he said the Mystery engine "BREATHS BETTER". They are the two most "Powerful Engines" that came off the Chevy Assembly Line. When Smokey Yunick passed away on May 9, 2001, Smokey's daughter invited me and my brother to come to his Shop as they let only a few people come to it. Roger could not make it, so Larry went with me, and we met my friend Ronald Northrip at the gate. We were standing outside Smokey's Shop in front of a set of windows waiting for his daughter to open the gate. As we were talking, I said to Ronald I can't wait to see the famous one of a kind "Dyno Machine" that Smokey built and put the famous Mystery Engine on it and Ronald said Ken see this big pipe buy us it is connected to the Dyno Machine for the exhaust. I looked in and saw the famous Dyno Machine. I asked Ronald what is that other pipe for that went up about 60 feet and he said Smokey produced his own electricity. He said the City of Daytona said they were going to raise the electric rates to all business and Smokey was at the meeting and said if you do that,

I will produce my own electricity and they all laughed. Smokey placed a propeller on top of the black iron pipe and supplied his own electricity. The gate opened and we received a personal tour looking at the car Smokey built and picked "Fireball Roberts" to drive it and he won races with it and then a professor from "Central Florida University" who stayed with Smokey for three months before he passed away to learn what this man new about engines and building race engines. He took us into Smokey's Office and some of his calculations were on the chalk board. He said Smokey designed the race pistons for GM and Intake Manifolds as we looked at them. He then showed us an Indy Race Car that Smokey built, and the small block Chevy engine and produced "1,000 HP" and it was "277 cui". He said no one has produced that kind of horsepower before. Then the Professor said next is a room where all the "FIRST ENGINES" that Chevy built came off the Assembly Line and they gave them to Smokey. He said there is "5 Codes" to get access to this room and Smokey was the only one that had the Codes. When we walked in it reminded me of "Reutimann Chevrolet Racing Team" as all the shelfs was wood. As I looked to the engine on the top left, it was the first "V8 Engine" Chevy built a 265-cui engine and then the 283-cui engine and the Big 348 – 409 W Series engines and then I asked the Professor a question. Where is the "427 cui Mystery Engine" and he said the one on the floor with no heads on it as it had aluminum plates on the block where the heads were. I asked the Professor what (RPM" was the Mystery Engine turning and he "CHOKED UP" and said I'm not at liberty to mention that. All the engines on both sides of the room and up high where all GM engines accept one and it was a "Ford Boss 427" and the reason, Smokey worked for Ford racing a couple of years. Next, we went to the Dyno room, and I got excited. The Professor stated this was the only one in the World that "Tested Everything" on an engine and Smokey designed it. In fact, Smokey gave it to the University to take and use. Smokey's daughter sold me Smokeys 4 huge books of his (Biography) and he was a "B – 17" Airforce Pilot and that is how he found Daytona from flying over it taking B-17's to Miami

Florida and he said that looks like where I want to live someday. As we were getting ready to leave, the Professor said there is only "ONE MYSTERY ENGINE" and it was Smokey Yunick's Engine. When we left next to Smokey's Shop in a Strip Mall was Ray Fox Racing and I walked into his office and introduced myself and I asked him what are you able to tell me about the Chevy 427 Mystery Engine. He said GM gave Smokey one and him and Rex White from NC one. He went on to say when we put it on a Dyno Machine the Power was "AWSOME" and he said GM called him and said Ray we want you to take your Race Car with the 427 Mystery Engine in it to Tx. for a straight away Race on a 1-mile stretch. He went on to say, Ford had their 427 and Chrysler had their 426 hemi and they could not stay up with the 427 Chevy Mystery Engine.

4. BUZZIE REUTIMANN 00

We met after I completed Orange "County Welding School" in 1965. In 1962 we watched the famous Reutimann 00 Race Car a 1957 Chevy with a 327 Corvette engine 360 hp written on the hood and the painting of the Red Woody the Woodpecker and he won most of the Races at Golden Gate Speedway in Tampa, Florida. When he came out of number 4 turn both wheels came off the ground when he punched it. When the "200 Lap Race "was held Buzzie would lap every car on the track except one, a 427 cui Ford 1956 Fairlane. Buzzie's Dad Emile was called Einstein, he was the first one to build a fuel Injection System for a Chevy V 8 engine. The Race Engines from California in 1963 could only get "375 cui" out of a 327-cui engine by boring it and stroking it. The Reutimann Racing Team engine they used for the Big Races was a small block 327 cui engine changed to over "400 cui" without using a boring machine. This was unheard of in the Racing World. In 1967 Buzzie Reutimann decided to go on the "NASCAR SUPERMODIFIED CIRCUIT" and I told him I would help him as I was a Certified Welder in Arc, Gas, Heliarc Welding. My assignment was all the Welding details on two "1947 Chevy

Coupes" that he was taking on the Circuit. Buzzie was a Believer and I always put God in all my work. I arc welded a gas tank for him and I put 40 lbs. air pressure on it to check for leaks and both tanks tested 100% no leaks, no one was able to do that at the time. Thank your Jesus, he gets the credit. One day Buzzie said Zifer I want you to build me a set of Headers for the engines and I will get the tubing for you. WOW, WOW, I always dreamed of doing this and now for a "FAMOUS RACING TEAM". WOW, WOW, Jesus is Powerful. This was my first set of "Exhaust Headers "that I built. The family loved the "Iskenderian Roller Camshafts". The Race Engine also had sitting on top of it "Hilborn Fuel Injection". The first year for Buzzie on the Big Circuit he finished the Season in the Northeast "First, Second, Third Place". One of the Great Race Drivers competing was using a Chevy 427 Mystery Engine and about the third year Buzzie was there. He was beating Buzzie by one fender length. When Buzzie came home after the Season he went to the Big Block 427 Chevy Mystery Engine. I was working on the Railroad at the time and rode the Train from Wildwood Florida to Middle Town New York. When I arrived at the Train Station, I looked up at the Skyscrapers and said I'm in another "WORLD" as I looked and stared at the huge buildings. The next day at the Farmhouse we went to the Barn where Buzzies Race Car was, and he said Ken I'm having some bad luck. I said what is it and he said a flat tire in one of the Races and the Big Block Chevy engine is running hotter than I like. I said Buzzie lets look at the Radiator. He said Ken they built a big one for me and it is still not at the Temperature I like it to be. As I looked, I said Buzzie remember the Big Block 348 and 409 engines they had the cowling from the Radiator run all the way to the front of the heads. Buzzie said build it for me Ziffer. We went to work and built it and the next day at the Races Buzzie "WON" the Race and when he came into the infield, I went up to the Race Car and said Bussie what was the Temperature and he said 212 degrees where I want it as it was running 230 degrees. Thank You Jesus. The "TWO 1947 CHEVY COUPES" took Buzzie Reutimann to the "NASCAR HALL OF FAME". I will never forget those days in my early 20's and I'm looking forward to meeting Buzzie again in a week as I'm writing this as me and Cathy are leaving our Log Cabin and headed to Florida to see Family and Friends. Today is May 6, 2021.

5. DR. LANCE WALLNAU

I met Dr. Lance Wallnau our Jewish friend personally at the Bible Museum in DC on Feb. 6, 2020 at 5: 33 pm just before he gave his speech at the evening meal. I thanked our Jewish friend for his "Boldness", and he was kind enough to let me get a picture with him. At 7:00 pm the Praise and Worship started with "Boldness" Songs and the message from Dr. Moore a Leader in the S. B. C. Denomination was about "Boldness". Conformation from the Holy Ghost. Also I met after the Service Dr. Russell D. Moore S.B.C. Leader and we had a picture taken. The Museum is two blocks from the Capital Building.

6. BOX 2 RADIO NETWORK – ELEVATED TALK AND INSPIRED MUSIC

On Feb.11, 2019 Quincy Burt and Whitney Ward interviewed me, and they asked me about the Documentary Wilderness Excursions of Florida that aired in Ga. two times in 5 counties. Also, they wanted to know more about me and the Supernatural Encounter I had with the Lord in 1998. The Holy Ghost spoke through me and I started out about my Salvation with our Jewish Rabbi, Yeshua / Jesus and about satan and his demons do not care who they attack and the Jesus Kingdom on earth. After the Interview they said Bro. Ken this aired around the "WORLD" in 46 Countries. It was an honor to be picked to be on their Radio Station in Ky. everyone needs to listen to them. Thank You Jesus.

7. RALPH BROGNE

I met him in 1974 as my Dad took me to his shop. Dad said Ken he was the only one that could "Weld" his kick stand on his motorcycle back in the 30's as it was pot metal. Mr. Ralph Brogne built Towers and sent them to Florida. He was a Machinist and Gunsmith and he came from Italy. As I talked with him he said Ken I can build any size caliber rifle from the smallest to the largest. He went on to say my Special Rifle is the "Brogne 6 x 61". He said it fires a 100 gr. Bullet and if you can hold a cigarette parallel to the earth at "300 yards" it will hit it. He said at 100 yards it will penetrate "1/4" Armored Still plate" and it will not ricochet off of metal. He took his ball point pen and clicked it open and said see the head of it, that is the biggest size of lead you will see when you hit a animal with it as it exploded. He said he "Bear Hunts" in British Columbia Canada. He went on to say the Federal Government Came to see him and wanted to buy the Rifle as they told him at the time they did not have a weapon that would kill instantly. They said we will use our name on the Rifle. Mr. Brogne said no deal if my name stamped on the barrel "Brogne" is removed. The deal did not take place. At the time a made arrangements for a Rancher in Florida and his name was Frank. He went hunting out to Montana and purchased one of a kind Rifles and it was delivered to his house. I saw Frank leaving a 7 Eleven Store in San Antonio, Florida a year later and I asked him did he kill any game with that rifle. He said when he went to Montana to Moose Hunt the Guide said that 100 gr. Bullet is not big enough. He did not know what this weapon brings down Bear. So the Deer Hunt the Guide said bring your rifle. Two Mule Deer Frank said were at least "300 yards" away on another Mountain Ridge and they were fighting. The Guide said take the one on the left. Frank said when he shot the deer dropped immediately. I said Frank where did you hit it at. He said the "Hind Quarters". Case dismissed. I have the Brogne 6 X 61 and planning on a "Bear Hunting Trip". Lets see what the Holy Ghost wants me to do. He uses me every where I go to do the Lords work.

DEDICATION

I dedicate this book to Jesus Christ of Nazareth and my wife Cathy and Grandson Zachary Zifer for inspiring me to write this book.

Ken and Cathy Zifer in Jerusalem outside the
Upper Room 2007

Ken Zifer Baptized by Pastor Allen Zifer July 2021

The Legend the only one in the World 2007

Zachary Zifer our grandson 2018

Pastor Obadiah Franklin

Ken and the BBQ Pit 2014

Ken Zifer at the Capital in DC blowing the Shofar 2019

Kenneth Zifer

www.ingramcontent.com/pod-product-compliance
Lightning Source LLC
Chambersburg PA
CBHW062037290426
44109CB00026B/2650